Mother OF THE Bride

REFRESHMENT AND WISDOM
FOR THE MOTHER OF THE BRIDE

Cheryl Barker

BroadStreet
P U B L I S H I N G

BroadStreet Publishing Group, LLC
Racine, Wisconsin, USA
BroadStreetPublishing.com

Mother of the Bride

Refreshment and Wisdom for the Mother of the Bride

ISBN-13: 978-1-4245-5236-8 (hardcover)
ISBN-13: 978-1-4245-5237-5 (e-book)

Cover and interior by Garborg Design Works at garborgdesign.com

Published in association with the literary agency of Credo Communications,
LLC, Grand Rapids, Michigan, credocommunications.net

Stock or custom editions of BroadStreet Publishing titles may be purchased in
bulk for educational, business, ministry, fundraising, or sales promotional use.
For information, please e-mail info@broadstreetpublishing.com.

Printed in China
16 17 18 19 20 5 4 3 2 1

For my daughters,
Kristin and Kelli,
and in memory of my mom,
Charlene Hoy.
You have each forever changed my life.
Love you always.

Contents

Wedding Vendor Worksheets

Acknowledgments

The road to holding this first published book in my hands has been a long but rewarding one. Many people have played a role in helping me reach this day, and I would like to offer my thanks to all.

First, I'm deeply grateful to my agent, Karen Neumair of Credo Communications, for believing in me and my book project and for persevering with me until God provided the perfect publishing home for my manuscript. Thank you for being such a great cheerleader, encourager, and help throughout the whole process. Thanks also to the team at Credo Communications for supporting Karen and me and for giving advice when needed.

My deepest gratitude also to BroadStreet Publishing for catching the vision for this book and for giving me, a first-time author, a chance to make my book-dream a reality. I'm so grateful for the opportunity to offer mothers of the bride the refreshment, encouragement, wisdom, and practical help they need on their MOB journeys. Thank you for making it possible. My appreciation to each team member who has worked so hard to make this book the best it can be.

I'd also like to thank those in the Fellowship of Christian Writers Online Critique Group who read my manuscript and helped me make this a better book. You know who you are. I so appreciated your feedback and continual encouragement. I also have special fondness and gratitude for the FCW members who gather each month for our meetings in Tulsa. The training I've received through our group has helped me grow in so many ways, and the support we offer one another is invaluable. Thanks so much for your friendship.

Another huge thanks goes to my prayer team. They've offered not only their prayers but much encouragement and support as well. So thank you to my husband, Don; my daughters, Kristin and Kelli; my dad, Duane; my sisters, Debbie, Janice, and Carolyn; my dearest friends Teri and Jeneal; and to my dear friend Nancy, who recently joined the team. I appreciate you all more than words can say. I also must mention my mom. She would be an important part of this prayer team, but God took her home just a few weeks before I signed with my agent. Mom was one of my biggest supporters and would be so proud to see my dream come true.

To Don, Kristin, and Kelli, thank you for being mine—my husband and my girls. Thank you for the bond we share and for our love that runs long and deep. To Shawn and Jake, thank you for loving my girls and for joining our crazy clan. You add so much to our family. And to my twin grandsons, Isaiah and James, I'm so grateful God blessed us with you. You are my newest joy and being your grandma is one of the best parts of my life. Kristin, I also want to thank you for reading my manuscript right alongside my critique group and offering input from a reader's perspective. I loved hearing your more personal comments. And Shawn and Kristin, thanks for acting as my tech team. You guys rock. Time and again you've come to my aid, and I deeply appreciate your help.

And finally and most importantly, I want to thank my Lord. Throughout this great adventure called life, which includes my writing journey, he has been my source of inspiration, my guide, my partner, and my strong support. He is my Savior and my greatest friend. Anything I've accomplished is because of him, and he is the one who keeps me persevering—in faith, in life, and in writing. Thank you, Lord. I will love you all of my days.

It's Official:
Let the Squeals Begin!

> "THE TRUE DELIGHT IS IN THE FINDING OUT"
> —ISAAC ASIMOV

Our lives changed forever one Friday evening in June. With the simple ring of a doorbell, a new era began. I glanced out the window and gasped.

"Don, it's Shawn!" I called out to my husband. Our daughter's boyfriend lived in Arkansas, nearly three hours away, and was scheduled to drive to Houston the next day where Kristin attended grad school. What was he doing at our home in Kansas?

The next instant, it dawned on me. This was *the* visit—the one we'd been anticipating.

"Shawn, what in the world?" Pretending ignorance, we continued with friendly small talk while waiting for him to reveal the real reason for his visit. Within minutes, he declared his intentions and asked for our blessing. He had it in a flash.

Then the squealing began. I admit I was the only one doing

it, but I couldn't help it. We had reached a milestone moment. Every mother who has a daughter looks forward to the day when a young man, more wonderful than she dared to hope for, arrives to ask for her little girl's hand in marriage. That day had finally come for me. I giggled. I gushed. And I squealed again.

A beaming Shawn chuckled at my reaction, taking pleasure in every second of it. He didn't realize until later that this would be the first of many shrieks of excitement he would hear from his future mother-in-law on his journey to the altar.

After my initial burst of celebration subsided, Shawn told us how he planned to propose to Kristin the next day. Dreaming of how happy she would be, I couldn't wait to see her. Then I remembered.

"Oh my gosh," I said. "I just realized something. My trip to Houston for Kristin's birthday has completely changed. Now we can go wedding gown shopping." As more squeals of delight ensued, Don and Shawn just shook their heads and smiled.

I didn't think it possible to get more excited than I already was until Shawn casually mentioned something else. Something that caught me by complete surprise. "I've got the ring out in the car. Want to see it?"

"What? Are you kidding? Of course I want to see it." Before I could squeal again, Don cut me short.

"Oh, Cheryl, I don't know." His eyes caught mine. "Do you really think Kristin would want you to see her ring before she does?"

His words jerked my runaway mother-of-the-bride ride to a stop. He was right. She would want to see it first. Painful though it was, I turned to Shawn and said, "I guess I better not. Darn ..." I sighed, the wind knocked out of my high-flying sails.

My disappointment didn't last long, though. After all, I wanted Kristin to experience the joy of showing me her ring for the first time. It would give me one more thing to look forward to when I arrived in Houston.

After another hour of happy conversation, Shawn decided to head to his sister's house in Tulsa. He planned to spend the night there so his trip to Houston the next day would be a little shorter.

As we began our good-byes, the phone rang. I checked the caller ID. It was our other daughter, Kelli.

"Oh no," I said. "It's Kelli! What am I going to say?"

"Don't tell her anything!" Shawn said. "Don't tell her I'm here—she'll figure out what's going on."

Somehow I managed to play it cool and keep it short as he and Don hung on my every word. I wrapped up the conversation as quickly as I could, and we all breathed a sigh of relief when I hung up. Then, like true conspirators, we laughed. "Won't it be fun to tell her about this later on?" I said, smiling.

As we walked Shawn out to his car, an amazing thought occurred to me. We were finally going to have a son. I shared my realization with the guys, my heart delighting in its newfound joy. *Thank you, God, for the wonderful man you brought into our daughter's life. Thank you for this newest member of our family.*

Soon after Shawn left, another reality intruded on my jubilant thoughts. The challenges that all parents face while planning a wedding would now be ours. How would we handle the expense and all the tasks involved? What about the decisions that would need to be made and the potential disagreements? Were we ready for the emotional roller coaster that awaited us?

If these questions sound familiar to you, you may have recently found out that your little girl is going to be a bride. Do you, by any chance, feel excited and terror stricken all at once? Don't worry—it's normal. You've just joined the ranks of Mother of the Bride.

Yes, you're an MOB now. Much awaits you over the next few months. You'll be traveling a sure-to-be challenging road much like the ones I traversed as a mother of the bride.

Join me, won't you, as I open a window into my MOB experiences and share some insights I gleaned along the way. I hope you'll feel refreshed and encouraged on your own MOB adventure as you experience mine with me. Be sure to follow the *Treat Yourself* suggestions at the end of each chapter. No one deserves them more than mothers of the bride.

And now? Here's to enjoying the journey!

A Gem for the Journey

Take time to delight in this milestone moment before getting distracted by details.

Treat Yourself

Call your sister or best friend and share the things you are most excited about. Do a little squealing!

Talk It Over

Ask your daughter what things she loves the most about her groom-to-be and then tell her the qualities you most admire in him. Thank God together for him.

A Bonus Wedding Planning Tip

Before the real planning begins, look at your calendar and consider upcoming projects, travels, and appointments. Also review normal items on your to-do list. Trim where you can by saying no to some tasks and delaying others. Try to keep your schedule as free as possible.

Your MOB Musings

As I begin my MOB journey, I'm happiest about and most looking forward to:

_____

_____

_____

_____

_____

_____

_____

_____

_____

_____

_____

_____

_____

_____

_____

_____

_____

_____

_____

First Things First: Start with Fun

You've made the calls. You've announced to all that your baby girl is getting married. What fun you've had spreading the news. Mother of the Bride, you may now be tempted to jump in and get down to the business of wedding planning, but let me encourage you to postpone it a little longer. The wedding-planning front will turn serious soon enough. For now, put first things first. Celebrate. Have some fun!

Lucky for me, I already had plans to visit my daughter when her marriage proposal changed our lives. No longer were we just an ordinary writer mom and hardworking grad student, we were now a scared-stiff-but-happy mother of the bride and a stars-in-her-eyes bride-to-be. And you can bet that with nearly six hundred miles between us and a ring just waiting to be flashed, I would have concocted a scheme to get to Kristin if one had not already been in the works. I had more squealing to do.

Five short days after Shawn put a ring on her finger, I loaded my car and headed for Houston. My fuel for the trip? Excitement. At least for the first portion of it. Funny how ten straight hours of driving can cripple an MOB's enthusiasm—not to mention her hips and legs. As Kristin came bounding out of her apartment to greet me, I peeled myself out of what had become my prison on wheels and gimped toward her, trying to smile and stifle groans simultaneously.

With left hand poised, she stood ready to dazzle me with her ring, while I, on the other hand, struggled to shake off my drive-induced stupor. My eyes had glazed over somewhere between Dallas and Houston, and I needed to rally to properly feast upon the engagement ring I'd been dying to see.

"There she is—there's our bride-to-be!" I said, trying to add some oomph to my voice as I made my way toward my firstborn. Squinting against the south Texas sunshine, I took her outstretched hand, mustered as much enthusiasm as I could, and said, "Oh, Kristin—how pretty! It's just beautiful!"

No doubt about it. The ring did sparkle with beauty. I just wish my first peek had come at a time when I possessed more energy. Still dazed by the drive, I didn't do justice to my new role as an elated mother of the bride.

No worries, though. After a good night's sleep, I jumped aboard the MOB thrill ride and promptly made up for lost time. The new day proved the ring to be beyond beautiful—worthy of my best squeals of delight, in fact. What better way to set the stage for fun than a gorgeous diamond ring and the dreams of a mother-daughter duo intent on planning the event of a lifetime?

After donning outfits cute enough for bridal shopping, we hurried out the door with an underlying sense of purpose highlighted by—you guessed it—pure glee. First stop? A bookstore. How could we proceed on Kristin's journey to the altar without a bridal planner?

Marching through the entryway of a nearby mega-bookstore, we surveyed the layout in seconds and then sprinted toward the wedding section. Kristin, already concerned about our expense for the upcoming affair, examined the beautiful planners but hesitated in making a choice.

"We don't have to buy one of these," she said. "I could make plans and take notes in a regular notebook. I don't need anything fancy."

"Oh, yes you do. I *want* you to have one. Which one do you like best?"

"But you're going to have so many other things to pay for. You don't need to get me one."

"Something like this will make planning much easier, though. Come on—it'll be fun. Let's get one!" I flashed her an encouraging smile and grabbed a quick hug. "In fact, I need some kind of planner for my own notes. Let's get yours and also find one for me. Maybe something small enough to fit in my purse."

With a burst of shopping-for-me-now energy, I scanned the aisles for notebooks or journals. Remembering I did indeed need to save where I could, I headed for the bargain section and soon discovered a perfect journal for my MOB needs. Not only was it a pretty shade of blue, one of the wedding colors Kristin had chosen, it was also inexpensive. Absolutely perfect. It made me giddy.

Who knew a little blue journal could elicit yet another squeal. I waited until we left the store, of course, but once outside, it escaped. We *both* had planners now. We were set and ready to roll.

With a list of bridal shops and our best-route strategies in hand, we embarked on the adventure all brides and their moms dream about for years—shopping for the dress. High spirits ruled the day as we visited bridal boutique after bridal boutique. From the royal treatment given by the sales clerks to the thrill of looking through the gowns to the pure delight of watching Kristin try on one gorgeous wedding dress after another, new and unforgettable memories became ours that day. Take it from me—every mother-daughter wedding-planning duo needs to shop for the gown on that first outing.

One of the best gifts you can give your daughter as a mother of the bride is to make her feel special. Let her see your joy at spreading the news of her engagement, and be sure she hears you rave about that new ring on her finger. Jump right in and kick off your journey together with bridal magazines and planners, and above all, get out there and start the quest for the dress. You might even want to host an engagement party for the soon-to-be "Mr. and Mrs."

These are the things that make it real. The things that bring it home. The first time you see your grown-up little miss looking back at you from a sea of white chiffon or beaded satin glory, indeed your heart will skip a beat. You'll find yourself blinking back tears. That elusive someday has suddenly become now. Your little girl—your jewel—is going to be a bride. You'll soon be giving her away.

If you find yourself feeling unparalleled happiness and unexpected sadness at the same time, don't worry—it's just one more stop on your MOB journey. Don't try to sidestep it. Embrace it. Then, Mother of the Bride, find your smile and get back to the fun!

A Gem for the Journey

Don't get bogged down in wedding planning too quickly. First have fun. Celebrate!

Treat Yourself

Gift yourself with a journal for your own notes. For extra fun, find it in one of the wedding colors.

Talk It Over

Talk with your husband, your best friend, or another loved one and find out what ideas he or she might have for ways to celebrate this exciting milestone. Carry out one idea now and save the others for times in the coming months when stress may mount.

A Bonus Wedding Planning Tip

Chronicle your adventure with photos—for yourself and for your daughter. Have a camera handy during all wedding planning sessions and outings.

Your MOB Musings

I can show our new Mr. and Mrs.-to-be how thrilled I am about their engagement by:

_____

_____

_____

_____

_____

_____

_____

_____

_____

_____

_____

_____

_____

_____

_____

_____

_____

3

Sleep–What's That? The MOB Brain Stuck in Overdrive

"A RUFFLED MIND MAKES A RESTLESS PILLOW."
—CHARLOTTE BRONTE

Your initial mother-daughter fling with fun has come and gone. The photos reveal only a fraction of the day's delight, but your heart captured the full picture. And now, Mother of the Bride, even though the first whirlwind of activity has subsided, your mind rushes on.

Chances are, you and your daughter brainstormed ideas for nearly every facet of the wedding during your celebratory first hours together. As a result, you may have come down with a bad case of MOB Brain Stuck in Overdrive.

No big surprise there. After all, it's your mission to see that your daughter's vision—yes, her dream—for her long-awaited wedding day comes true. I know. I've been there. Twice now, actually. My younger daughter, Kelli, made me an MOB three years after Kristin did.

After two stints in the making-dreams-come-true department, I can assure you that such a lofty mission seriously impedes anything resembling a good night's sleep. The endless details of planning a dream come true can overwhelm the mind of almost any woman. In fact, once she becomes a mother of the bride, I doubt a woman exists who can turn off her details switch and get a solid night's sleep.

Anything out of the ordinary in my life, wedding related or not, launches my mind into overdrive and keeps me thinking night and day. My problem isn't falling asleep. It's staying asleep. As soon as I wake up the tiniest bit, my thoughts ignite. Slipping back into slumber becomes a lost cause. Imagine how a wedding—the mother of all sleep disturbances—affected *this* mother of the bride.

From attire to décor, from menu to vendors—each detail waited its turn to sabotage any chance I had for a full night of refreshing sleep. I could have tried counting sheep, but with a wedding on the brain, they soon would have resembled bridesmaids or bolts of tulle.

On the days I had the misfortune of waking in the wee hours of the morning, my groggy MOB musings went something like this:

What is it that's going on? Oh yeah, the wedding ... I need to have Kristin look for more of those blue pillar candles. Maybe one of the Houston Hobby Lobbys will have them. I don't know what we'll do if they don't ... I guess Shawn could check in Fayetteville. Wonder how he'd feel about going to Hobby Lobby ... Guess we'll find out if it's true love or not.

Good grief, I've gotta get back to sleep ... Oh yeah, we're gonna need white extension cords. Hate to have to buy those. Maybe we could borrow some. Let's see, who could I email?

Sure hope I get an e-mail back from the caterer today. Makes me nervous not hearing anything yet ... At least I heard from the cake lady. So glad she still had an open slot on Kristin's wedding weekend. We really need that to-die-for cake since we're just doing the light buffet.

Wonder how Shawn will want his groom's cake designed ... Guess I don't care as long as it's chocolate ... Can't wait to have that yummy cake. I want a piece of both, though ... Surely the mother of the bride deserves two pieces of cake.

Oh Lord, please help me—I've GOTTA get back to sleep ... also gotta get another chance to go shopping. Need to find my dress now ... Wish that one at Dillard's would go on sale. Guess I could open a charge account and get a discount that way ... but it really oughta be on sale first ... It was perfect.

Sure would like to find the perfect wedding album for Kristin and Shawn ... I know exactly what she'd like. Maybe I should try the little gift shop here in town ... who knows, they might have just what I'm looking for.

And we need to look for flowers soon too. Sure wish Kristin lived closer ... Wish at least one of us lived where they're getting married.

I wish—I wish I could go back to sleep! Lord, please, please help me get back to SLE-E-EP.

And so it would go. Each day I'd tell myself I couldn't keep this up for the next several months, that I'd either go crazy or collapse from sleep deprivation. But sheer willpower didn't do the trick. Early mornings still found me making mental lists or remembering yet another phone call I needed to make. The mother of the bride, ever on duty ...

Mother of the Bride, your early morning MOB sleep-robbing thought fests may touch on slightly different issues than mine did, but if you're actively involved in helping your daughter plan her wedding, it's safe to assume you're losing sleep on a regular basis. I wish I could tell you there's an easy answer for this Brain-Stuck-in-Overdrive MOB dilemma, but I'm afraid there's not. At least not one I've discovered.

I *can* hold out hope, though. Believe me, when you're finally tired enough, you'll snooze like Sleeping Beauty clear through till morning. You'll wake up refreshed, almost giddy over your good night's rest. Then you'll ask God to grace your world soon with such sweet slumber again.

In the meantime, keep a small spiral notebook, a pen, and a little flashlight on your bedside table, and jot down things as they come to you. After that, all you can do is hang on for the MOB Brain-Stuck-in-Overdrive ride. It's a wild one!

A Gem for the Journey

Give your brain a break—don't try to remember all the details. Write everything down, then relax.

Treat Yourself

Start that novel you'd like to read. Give your mind a place to retreat.

Talk It Over

Ask your daughter if details, worries, or concerns are interrupting her sleep. Talk about each one and discuss ways to help alleviate these stressors. End your conversation with a prayer, asking God to help you both.

A Bonus Wedding Planning Tip

Implement whatever organizational system works best for you, but then be sure to review your to-do list at least once a week. You don't want to miss a time-sensitive deadline. As a backup measure, record those deadlines on your calendar as well. Also, if you're working with a very small budget, go ahead and make a list of items you might be able to borrow.

Your MOB Musings

The concerns that rob me of sleep most often are:

_____

_____

_____

_____

_____

_____

_____

_____

_____

_____

_____

_____

_____

_____

_____

_____

_____

_____

_____

_____

When God Is Your Wedding Planner: Finding the Ultimate Coordinator

"And my God shall supply all your need according to His riches in glory by Christ Jesus." —The apostle Paul, in Philippians 4:19 NKJV

It's funny how the mother of the bride's life undergoes an overnight transformation. For me, day-to-day issues that cried importance before our daughters' engagements lost much of their urgency once their boyfriends popped the question. Other projects and plans got pushed to the back burner of my mind while wedding plans grabbed center stage.

Once the dates were set, prudence demanded action. We had to move quickly if we wanted to secure the sites and vendors needed to fulfill the hopes of our daughters and soon-to-be sons-in-law. It was time to get to work. Time to put feet to the myriad of details cluttering my poor MOB brain.

In Kristin and Shawn's case, we all lived in different states, further complicating the issues at hand. To top it off, they decided to tie the knot in yet another state. The reason for such madness? They wanted to get married at The University of Tulsa, where they had met and attended school together. I had to admit it made perfect sense, especially since they both had ties to the university's chapel. Kristin had been the church accompanist, and Shawn had been involved in student leadership.

Many would say we needed a wedding planner, a professional coordinator to handle the unique challenges we faced. Realistically, though, that wasn't in our budget. As mother of the bride, I would need to rise to the occasion if our dream of giving Kristin and Shawn a beautiful wedding celebration to remember was to become a reality.

I immediately turned to the Lord, my best friend and constant companion in life. He walks with me through everything, whether in the ordinary or extraordinary, whether in joy or in sorrow. Not only do I love and worship him each day, he's the one I turn to in time of need. He's my heavenly Father. My faith in God has always been the strong foundation of my life, and this adventure would be no exception. God became our wedding planner.

I asked the Lord to guide Kristin and Shawn in all their decisions, and I stayed in constant touch with him, knowing that he, the maker of the world, could handle the overwhelming task before us. I recorded our needs in my prayer journal and took each issue to him in prayer. As the answers came, I entered those as well, rejoicing in his goodness to us.

In fact, our heavenly wedding planner blessed us financially in ways an earthly one could never have. Not only did he provide relief by stretching our dollars through lots of sale items, some services provided as gifts, and the gift of a car, he also provided extra finances through Shawn's parents' contributions, additional income, and the completion of our mortgage payments.

Mother of the Bride, if you ask God to become *your* wedding planner, not only will he help you stretch dollars, but he will also give guidance in making decisions, whether large or small. For example, in a city where we were unfamiliar with the vendors we needed to book, God directed us to the perfect reception site, an excellent and reasonably priced caterer, and a baker whose wedding cake and groom's cake crowned the celebration with a taste of heaven. The Lord led in every decision, from where to have the bridesmaids' luncheon and which hotel to book to how to decorate and what to give as our wedding gift. Like in other areas of my life, I found that no concern was too small to take to God in prayer.

When problems arise, Mother of the Bride—and they always do when planning a wedding—God will provide either solutions or the grace needed to handle the situations. For example, before Kristin finally wore her bridal gown down the aisle, excitement turned to distress three different times. Serious dress dilemmas presented themselves, including a dry-cleaning nightmare and a last-minute alteration challenge. Throw in a crisis with the wedding invitations and an unexpected need for printing services just days before the wedding, and you have the makings for major meltdowns. I'll share more details in later chapters, but for now let me assure you that our heavenly wedding planner propped us up each and every time.

Yes, God helped us rise to the occasion. He walked with us through it all, from the first thrilling hours of searching for the perfect bridal gown to those last-minute, panic-stricken moments when something went wrong. Most importantly, he helped us maintain good relationships day in and day out while navigating the emotional minefield also known as wedding planning.

In addition, God blessed us with the very things I asked of him. The Bible says, "For we have all received from his fullness one gracious gift after another" (John 1:16 NET). And that's exactly what God did for us. He graciously blessed. It was as if he celebrated with us as he granted good health, nice weather, a good turnout, a great family reunion, and a wonderful wedding celebration for our precious daughter and the love of her life.

All of this should come as no surprise, though. We had the ultimate wedding planner in our corner—the Lord God himself. After all, his Son Jesus is described in Scripture as the bridegroom of a radiant bride, the church, and heaven itself as the site for his wedding supper. God is certainly no stranger to wedding planning.

As always, my heavenly Father proved to be not only my faithful provider as I brought my needs to him but also my loving companion. He showed me that he will indeed walk with me through every situation—even something as detailed and froufrou as wedding planning.

MOB, on your journey as mother of the bride, I guarantee you will have needs of your own. You may discover you need a wedding planner much like the one we had. You're in luck. Have I got the guy for you!

A Gem for the Journey

God is willing and able to help you plan the perfect celebration for the jewel of your heart and her groom.

Treat Yourself

Go to the spot where you most easily sense God's presence. Spend some time basking in his love.

Talk It Over

Spend some time talking to God. Ask him to guide you as you help your daughter plan her big day. Tell him all your concerns and also thank him for the many blessings in your life.

A Bonus Wedding Planning Tip

As soon as the date and site for the wedding have been determined, have the bride and groom help select a photographer. Many photographers book weddings up to a year in advance. Act quickly to secure your top choice. If the expense of a professional photographer is a major concern, consider asking a friend, relative, or acquaintance who loves photography to serve as your photographer. She might offer her services as a gift to the bride and groom, or perhaps you could barter with her in some way. Just be sure to review samples of her work before securing her as your photographer. You don't want to make a mistake with these once-in-a-lifetime photos.

Your MOB Musings

Some ways my faith has already helped me as an MOB and other ways I'd like my faith to impact my MOB journey are:

_____

_____

_____

_____

_____

_____

_____

_____

_____

_____

_____

_____

_____

_____

_____

_____

_____

_____

_____

5

Whose Wedding Is This? Finding a Balance

"A LITTLE CONSIDERATION, A LITTLE THOUGHT
FOR OTHERS, MAKES ALL THE DIFFERENCE."
—EEYORE, IN A. A. MILNE'S *WINNIE THE POOH*

It doesn't take long for the inevitable to happen. Differences of opinion—and big ones at that—lie in wait just over the threshold of the wedding planning minefield. The soon-to-be Mr. and Mrs. casually drop a bombshell that leaves her parents trying not to overreact yet having no choice but to say, "You wanna do *what*?"

The conversation that follows will most likely end with the newly engaged daughter saying, "Whose wedding is this anyway? It's not your decision. It's *our* wedding." The mother of the bride, still very much a parent, then dishes up some perspective. "That may be true, but remember—we're the ones throwing the party. We have some dreams and desires too."

What happens next may determine the prevailing atmosphere

for the next several months, and the MOB's communication style will set the tone for it all. Honest, gentle communication from the mother of the bride can make a difference when problems arise, and it can be especially helpful in striking a balance when the "whose wedding is this anyway" scenario pops up.

Hopefully, both couples will recognize the need for some give and take. If they're wise, each will determine to always listen when a differing viewpoint surfaces and to be ready to make some concessions.

Our first difference of opinion with Kristin and Shawn occurred fewer than forty-eight hours after he proposed. We had already weathered—like regular troopers—news of their desire to hold the wedding in a state where none of us lived. The next little bombshell, however, baffled us.

"Mom, Shawn and I made a few decisions today about the wedding," Kristin said during the first of many phone conversations we had with six hundred miles between us.

"Oh, really? What did you decide?" I said, with the phone wedged between my head and shoulder as I folded some towels.

"Well, we think it would be a good idea to have just one attendant each."

I dropped a towel in midfold and jerked to attention. "What? Just one? Why do you want to do that? That's not what you've talked about before."

"I know, but it'll be easier this way."

While some may not consider one attendant each a big deal, this announcement shocked and saddened me—and also Don when I shared the news with him. It was a complete reversal of previous desires we'd heard Kristin express. Now instead of asking several of her college friends and also Kelli to serve as bridesmaids, she planned to have only a maid of honor—Kelli.

Reading between the lines, I suspected Kristin and Shawn thought this was the easiest way of dealing with the dilemma of who to ask. We couldn't imagine that she and Shawn would later be happy with this decision, and we knew we wouldn't. It didn't fit Kristin's personality, and it wasn't at all what we had imagined for our little girl's big day.

Don and I agreed that we should ask them to reconsider. We didn't want to differ with them so early in the game, but this seemed too important. Since I could express our thoughts as carefully as possible in an e-mail, the following arrived in Kristin's inbox just two nights after she officially became a bride-to-be:

Hey Kristin, Dad wanted me to tell you his thoughts about your one attendant each decision. Rather than broach it over the phone, I decided to e-mail so you could think about it a little more and talk it over with Shawn before responding. We don't want to cause stress or have you feel like we're arguing—it's just discussion, a sharing of thoughts and feelings.

Dad was let down and puzzled by your plan—and I felt the same way. To us, it takes away from the celebration, excitement, and fun of the whole thing. It seems kind of sad to us. Dad would like to see more buildup before you come down the aisle, and with just one bridesmaid that wouldn't happen. I think he's very proud of you and loves you and wants to give you a wonderful wedding.

Also, it's always important to think of others' feelings. I'm sure your friends would be disappointed at not getting to share in the joy and excitement of everything with you. Friendship has always been very important to you, and just a couple of months ago you were telling me about everyone you wanted as bridesmaids when you got married. So now we're puzzled by this.

I realize you may not see these friends much after the wedding, but that's how life works. It doesn't make the friendships any less important or treasured. As you grow older, you'll see how your early-in-life friendships hold a very important place in your heart and memories. So ... keep on making memories with your friends as long as you can.

On a more practical note, it would also add to the color and beauty of the scene to have more attendants—but you know I'm not an expert on making things look beautiful.

Mainly, we just want to give you a happy, memorable, beautiful wedding celebration. We wouldn't want you to regret, before or after the wedding, not having your friends up there with you or feeling like things weren't quite as nice as you would have liked after all.

So, just hear our hearts on this. Think about it a little more and consider all these thoughts. We want planning your wedding to be fun, so we'll support whatever you and Shawn finally decide. Just be willing to discuss things and hear different points of view ... A little stress is to be expected when planning a wedding—it goes with the territory. If we accept that, we can express views and still have fun, whatever decisions are finally made. Really, I want it to be fun!! I'm looking forward to the whole mother-of-the-bride thing—and making it fun for you to be the bride!! Okay??!!

We love you both,

Mom for Dad, too

As I waited to hear back from Kristin, I prayed that our message to them would be well received. By the next time she and I spoke, they had changed their minds. We went from a maid of honor and best man to a full slate of five attendants each. Kristin and Shawn were happy, we were happy, and plans for the celebration gained exciting momentum.

Even though the bridal party decision turned out the way we hoped, it was just the first of many issues we discussed. Kristin and Shawn—and later Kelli and her fiancé, Jake, when it was their turn—made several choices that we wouldn't have personally made.

You, too, Mother of the Bride, will have differences of opinion with your bride and her groom during the months of planning ahead, and most decisions will go their way. After all, it *is* their wedding. Remember, though, as the parents, it's okay to share your desires on the things that are important to you.

So, MOB, how do you find a balance when your desires collide with that of your daughter and her beloved? Three Cs can help diffuse the problems lying in wait for you on the wedding planning minefield: Consideration, Communication, and Compromise.

With an honest and gentle communication style, you can employ these strategies and set a happy tone for your family's upcoming wedding-planning days. Remember, in the words of Eeyore, "A little Consideration, a little Thought for Others, makes all the difference."

A Gem for the Journey

Honest but gentle communication from the beginning is key.

Treat Yourself

Take the bride out for a cup of coffee or yummy dessert and catch up on some girl talk—something other than wedding details if possible!

Talk It Over

Ask your daughter what her deepest desires are for her wedding and suggest that she ask her groom about his if she hasn't already. Share some of your desires as well and then together discuss what you can do to help at least a few of these dreams come true.

A Bonus Wedding Planning Tip

Surprise your daughter with some bridal magazines and then look through them together. This will help you get a sense of her likes and dislikes and enable you to make helpful suggestions. Pinterest is also a great place to look for ideas and create wedding-themed boards together. You can check out my wedding boards at pinterest.com/cherbark.

Your MOB Musings

My deepest desires for my precious girl's wedding are:

_____

_____

_____

_____

_____

_____

_____

_____

_____

_____

_____

_____

_____

_____

_____

_____

_____

_____

To Have and To Hold...
Until She Gets Married

"LOVING SOMEONE IS SETTING THEM FREE,
LETTING THEM GO." —KATE WINSLET

You've spent her whole life holding her. Whether cradled in your arms as a baby or wrapped in your embrace as a young woman, she's been yours to have and to hold, Mother of the Bride—until now. Now the time has come to let her go, to let her begin her own family and pledge her allegiance to another. It's a bittersweet time, to be sure.

A few years ago, my husband and I embarked on this letting-go journey for the second time. When Kelli got engaged, I knew our "having and holding her" days were numbered, and I wondered if it would be any easier this time around. Of course, it wasn't. The ache of letting go arrived, unavoidable and sure.

Fortunately, Mother of the Bride, letting go of our daughters is a process that begins long before wedding day dawns. I'm glad we get to take it a step at a time. It begins with small steps, leaving them as babies in someone else's care for an hour or two. But then before we know it, we're saying our good-byes at an out-of-town university and making them promise to come home soon for a visit.

The ring on the finger, however, signals that the final phase of "Operation Letting Go" has begun. From the time our daughters' boyfriends ask for our blessings to the moment we hear the minister say, "Who gives this woman?" new steps of release wait to be mastered. A new dynamic must test its wings.

During Kristin's engagement, several changes occurred in the final leg of the letting-go journey, each one a natural part of the process but a challenge to adjust to nonetheless.

First, Shawn became her go-to man for everything, her expert advisor in every situation. Whether choosing a cold medicine or deciding wedding details, Kristin's standard mantra became, "Let me see what Shawn thinks." And even though I welcomed groom participation in the wedding planning, I admit I eventually thought, *Can't we decide anything on our own anymore?* This dark-haired, six-foot-four force, otherwise known as my future son-in-law, had captivated my daughter, heart and soul. A good thing, to be sure, but an adjustment for me, her *former* expert advisor.

Kristin's coming-home visits changed as well. No longer did we have exclusive claim to her time or destination. Since she and Shawn lived eight hours apart, she naturally wanted to spend as much time with him as possible. This even included her Christmas break. Yes, *Christmas.* Oh, we got her for the holiday, but it was still difficult to sacrifice any time together. I know now that it was good preparation for the changes future holidays would hold.

Then came the issue of a new family. Not only did "Operation

Letting Go" involve sharing our dearly loved daughter with a soon-to-be husband, but it also required sharing her with another family. We welcomed Shawn into our happy little clan with joy, but the thought of a different family claiming our girl as one of their own hurt a little. It's one thing to welcome a son-in-law and quite another to give up a daughter, even to a terrific family like Shawn's.

Talk about a range of emotions. At one end of the spectrum, I felt deep gratitude for the wonderful in-law family Kristin would have, but the opposite end—jealousy—didn't look so pretty. That's right, the green-eyed monster tried to sneak in.

My mind raced with thoughts of the changes ahead. *Kristin might call Shawn's parents Mom and Dad ... And they'll get to see them more since they live nearby. They'll probably even be the favorite grandparents.*

Unhealthy thinking without a doubt, but fear can do that to people. Yes, I was afraid. Afraid of being replaced. Afraid of slipping to second place.

Add to that Kristin showing Shawn's parents special consideration at times while being somewhat insensitive to us, and jealousy crept in again. My nephew's wife, calling on her own experience, gave me a new vantage point, though. "Kristin's just trying to fit into Shawn's family and please them, but she feels safe with you—she knows she can let her guard down." After hearing that, I felt less hurt and more sure of my place in her heart.

As I considered my jealousy issue, I knew being jealous was wrong and could only cause harm. I decided to douse that fire each and every time it tried to flare—a decision in everyone's best interest. If a spark of jealousy ignited, I took it to God in prayer, asking him to help me let it go.

When Kelli got married, I experienced those reluctant-to-share-my-daughter feelings all over again. I guess they can't be avoided. Let's just say this mixed bag of in-law family emotions falls into the MOB happy-yet-sad-at-the-same-time category. Once again, it's completely normal.

And what about the final letting go—the wedding day itself? I'm afraid that chain of emotions can't be stopped. We might be able to curb them for a while, but eventually they'll catch up with us. My meltdown at Kristin's wedding came during the father-daughter dance.

I held it together during the ceremony when Don walked our little girl—our firstborn—down the aisle and gave her away. I held it together as I heard Kristin pledge her undying love and loyalty to Shawn and begin a new family unit. I even held it together—and in fact, felt great joy—as I watched the slideshow of Kristin's and Shawn's lives. But the tears finally fell when Don joined Kristin on the dance floor, just the two of them, just a daddy and his daughter. So many memories. So much emotion.

When your final letting go happens, Mother of the Bride—when you think your place in her life has forever changed—I think you'll find she still needs you. Kristin needed me even before leaving the reception. While changing to leave for the honeymoon, she couldn't find a needed item. So who was called on to save the day? That's right. And find the item, I did. And I admit—it felt satisfying to still be taking care of my now-married daughter. My mom spot was secure.

So, MOB, whether it's a cry for help before she leaves the party or a phone call from the airport as she returns from her honeymoon—even though she's a married woman now—you'll still have those precious mother-daughter moments to have and to hold ... until forever.

A Gem for the Journey

Let go of your daughter with grace and you'll find her calling on you with joy.

Treat Yourself

Call, e-mail, or get together with the mother of the groom and share some of the wedding details. Treat yourself to a new friendship!

Talk It Over

Talk with your husband about any letting-go struggles you're having and ask him how he's doing. If you're not married, share your feelings with your mom, your sister, or your best friend.

A Bonus Wedding Planning Tip

Include the groom's mom in some aspect of the wedding planning. Ask her to provide the wedding card box for the gift table, enlist her help in decorating the reception site, or ask her advice when selecting the groom's cake.

Your MOB Musings

The hardest parts of letting go for me are:

_____

_____

_____

_____

_____

_____

_____

_____

_____

_____

_____

_____

_____

_____

_____

_____

_____

_____

Keeping Secrets:
Fun but Serious Business

"THE HUMAN HEART HAS HIDDEN TREASURES, /
IN SECRET KEPT, IN SILENCE SEALED; / THE THOUGHTS,
THE HOPES, THE DREAMS, THE PLEASURES, /
WHOSE CHARMS WERE BROKEN IF REVEALED."
—CHARLOTTE BRONTE, IN "EVENING SOLACE"

Keeping secrets. It's one of the most overlooked challenges a mother of the bride faces. Engagement secrets, wedding-planning secrets, shower and honeymoon secrets—all there, testing her ability to keep highly classified information secure behind her dying-to-tell-somebody lips. If she fails this test, she might not be trusted in future situations.

Mother of the Bride, if you hope to succeed in keeping secrets, you must adopt a nonchalant demeanor, suppressing the secrets at all times. If the glee of your hidden knowledge makes it to your eyes, you're a goner. The goods—or a thinly veiled version of them—will come tumbling out as curious listeners ply you with questions.

My best tip? Avoid eye contact when conversations turn to topics you need to sidestep. I learned this early when tasked with keeping major secrets before my daughters officially became brides-to-be.

We had plans to visit Kelli the day after Shawn appeared at our door, seeking our blessing before proposing to Kristin. When he heard we'd be with Kelli the next day, he swore us to secrecy until he could ask Kristin to be his wife. I was to wait for Kristin's call before squealing my joy to Kelli.

The next day as we shopped and had lunch together, I kept my guard up and my eyes ready to look away if Kelli asked about Kristin or Shawn. Like a kid waiting until it's time to open presents, I checked my phone every few minutes, making sure I hadn't missed a call.

Finally the call came when Kelli and I were in line at Bath and Body Works. Surrounded by other women at the checkout, I answered the phone. "Hey, Kristin," I said in the most casual tone I could manage. Staying subdued and vague in my replies so Kristin could surprise Kelli, I said, "Kelli's right here. You wanna talk to her?"

As soon as Kelli uttered her first syllable of glee, I joined in with my signature squeal and proclaimed to all standing nearby, "My daughter just got engaged!"

After our sister shoppers thrilled in the moment with us, I told Kelli the full story. In an instant, the delight of a secret revealed made it worth the excruciating hours of forced silence. My MOB duty had required painful self-control, but the result left me smiling.

When Kelli's turn came to get engaged, I had to endure a secret-keeping marathon. No simple overnight wait to set my lips free this time. Months before Jake proposed, Kelli let their plans slip in a phone conversation. They hoped to get engaged that summer. I, like any good mother of the bride, flew straight into excited mode—until she charged me with keeping it a secret.

"Can't I at least tell your dad—and maybe Teri?" I couldn't bear to wait for months without sharing the news with my husband and one of my girlfriends. Lucky for me, Kelli agreed to let them in on the secret.

The secret keeping intensified after Jake pulled Don aside one evening and shared his plans to propose to Kelli on her birthday. Now that the coming engagement was certain, how would I ever wait two more weeks? By the time she called the night of her birthday, I was ready to burst. I waited for her to say the words, squealed my delight and demanded details, and then begged for permission to spread the news. After getting the go-ahead, I didn't let my phone cool off for the next hour. Talk about sweet relief.

The relief didn't last long, however. With both couples, soon other news had to be guarded. I couldn't let any talk—or photos—of bridal attire come near the grooms. At the same time, I withheld news of Shawn's wedding gift of bridal jewelry for Kristin. Good thing he gave it to her early, before she insisted we shop for it ourselves.

Mother of the Bride, also expect other secrets to reach your ears as the wedding day draws near. As you keep all aspects of the wedding progressing on schedule, much like a juggler moving several balls through the air with precision timing, you'll be privy to information about gifts, bridal showers, bachelorette parties, and maybe even the honeymoon. Guarding fun secrets actually provides a welcome change of pace.

But let's not forget the more serious secrets. For example, the bride and groom don't need to know the price tag on everything—nor do friends and family. Our bridal couples knew the cost of major items because they helped research vendors and make decisions, but we were careful not to announce a running total every time expenses mounted. Better to downplay the cost publicly than to sap the bride and groom's joy.

Even more important to keep private are criticisms that will only cause division if repeated. The Bible says, "Whoever would foster love covers over an offense, but whoever repeats the matter separates close friends" (Proverbs 17:9 NIV). No need to tell your daughter about a negative comment you overheard about her groom or to pass along stories of how someone hurt your feelings in a matter concerning the wedding. Also, fears—like mine—of slipping to a less important place in your daughter's life or of losing her to another family are best kept to yourself or confessed only to your closest confidantes. And the things your daughter has designated for your ears only? Guard them at all times.

Keeping secrets can be part of the fun, but at the same time it's serious business. As you prove your ability to zip your lips about secret wedding details, MOB, you lay the groundwork for trust when your daughter and son-in-law want to share private information in the future.

One day, you won't only be the mother of the bride—you'll be the mother of the couple. Will they be able to trust you with their secrets? Remember, some of them may require marathon endurance. Every secret you keep now provides good training ground.

Whatever the situation, now or in the future, determine to be a good secret keeper. The challenges will be great, but the benefits of a sweet relationship will put a smile on your face—and theirs.

A Gem for the Journey

Like the scriptural principle, prove faithful in the small things and you'll be trusted with much in the future.

Treat Yourself

All this secret keeping calls for some chocolate. Go ahead and indulge—I won't tell!

Talk It Over

Ask your daughter and future son-in-law what information about the wedding or their lives they currently consider top-secret and then assure them that their secrets will be safe with you.

A Bonus Wedding Planning Tip

Some things are not a secret. When you're asked, have a list handy of the bride's choices in china, dinnerware, crystal, and flatware as well as her color schemes for her new home.

Your MOB Musings

The secrets that will be the hardest for me to keep will probably be:

_____

_____

_____

_____

_____

_____

_____

_____

_____

_____

_____

_____

_____

_____

_____

_____

Mother of the Bride: No Job for a Weakling

"WISH ME COURAGE AND STRENGTH AND A
SENSE OF HUMOR—I WILL NEED THEM ALL."
—ANNE MORROW LINDBERGH

"Kristin, you're never gonna believe this," I said into the phone, my voice croaking each word. "I'm getting sick."

"Mom, you can't get sick *now*. We have to work on wedding details before I head back to Houston. I've got appointments made in Tulsa for the next two days." She paused and then said, "You'll just have to push through."

My squeals of delight at becoming a mother of the bride just six weeks earlier now turned to a weary sigh. She was right. I didn't have a choice. Maybe I would feel better the next day.

No overnight cure came, however. But push through I would. I packed my bag and pointed my car toward Tulsa with the resolve of a soldier on a mission. No, make that a mother of the bride on a mission—Mission Secure-the-Vendors.

Two days later and with no voice left, I'd accomplished most of the task, but my health hadn't fared so well. Back at home and feverish, I headed to the doctor. This MOB gig was no job for a weakling.

Though I longed to curl up on the sofa for days, my mother-of-the-bride responsibilities wouldn't allow it. With a day of rest and fewer than forty-eight hours of antibiotics in my system, I took off for Tulsa again, this time with Don in tow, to meet Kristin and Shawn for a day of cake tasting. Crazy? Yes. But it had to be done while she was available.

That was the week I learned that MOBs do what they've gotta do—whether feeling healthy and happy or puny and pathetic. Who knew mothers of the bride needed the physical stamina of Olympic champions?

Granted, my situation was unusual. Not every mom lives hundreds of miles from her daughter. Not every mom has to wedding plan during brief windows of opportunity. Not every mom has to push through.

But, every mother of the bride does face wedding-planning feats that would send most men to their knees. The shopping alone presents unparalleled challenges. And for moms like me who don't live near retail meccas and who have long lists to conquer during each trip, shopping feels more like a triathlon than a girls' day out.

Not only do MOBs help shop for the bridal gown and bridesmaids' dresses, they also must find the perfect mother-of-the-bride attire. Add to that all the necessary accessories for themselves and the bride, and their days on the run keep multiplying.

Shopping for wedding décor and everything needed to throw the party of a lifetime also requires long hours and strong legs, especially since any self-respecting MOB goes to great lengths to snag the best possible deals. Mother of the Bride, why not ask a friend to accompany you on such missions. After all, immediate family members might balk at running the marathon needed.

When the wedding weekend arrives, MOB, your physical challenges will reach new heights. Days of nonstop activity, including playing hostess to out-of-town family members, will find you on duty from first light until midnight. How well I remember my one reprieve—the rehearsal dinner. Not my area. Not my responsibility. Just pure bliss.

Of course, physical stamina is only one kind of strength you'll need, Mother of the Bride. Different weddings present different challenges.

I've had friends whose daughters gave them only two or three months to pull together their fairy-tale weddings. Mental strength, also known as nerves of steel, must then be displayed. But even nerves of steel can become frayed. At times, my friends looked like the proverbial deer in the headlights. One even admitted to a good old-fashioned crying jag.

Unshakable nerves also come in handy when the inevitable crisis presents itself. Whether you, MOB, have a problem like we did with the bridal gown or the invitations, or whether any number of other things happens, your nerves need to be strong enough to carry you as well as the bride.

Along with physical stamina and nerves of steel, you'll also need every ounce of emotional strength you can muster as you weather the choppy waters of wedding planning. Most mothers of the bride face some stressful expense-related conversations with their husbands, and every MOB deals with the emotional undercurrent of forging relationships with the groom and his family. Trying to be sensitive to them as well as your own family and friends, MOB, will keep you walking an unfamiliar tightrope.

The wedding planning conversations between you and your daughter—the star of the show—can stress the emotions like no other, though. The hormonal factor alone is a ticking time bomb. With PMS and bridal jitters on one hand and menopausal mood swings and irritability on the other, a few clashes are bound to happen.

Some mothers and daughters will have different approaches to wedding planning. Conflicts may occur before discovering how to best work together. It happened to Kelli and me. We eventually found it helpful to talk about the problem and share our feelings honestly, even though it meant a few tears. We were then able to put the unhappiness behind us and move forward with a new sensitivity to each other's feelings.

Other emotional challenges may sneak up on you, Mother of the Bride, when issues of letting go and shifting loyalties arise. Also, certain decisions regarding the wedding have more emotional impact than others. You may expect the wedding to take place in a certain city or church. You may know the perfect person to officiate the ceremony, or you may hope your daughter will wear the veil or slip or necklace you wore on your own wedding day. When she decides differently, your heart may ache a little.

Other people can also hurt your feelings. You might overhear someone criticizing your plans for the reception or be deeply disappointed by someone who doesn't come to the wedding. Sometimes a family member may fail to give the bride and groom a gift. It's best to forgive these hurts and concentrate instead on all the blessings surrounding the big event.

These upsets combined with the stress of regular life can

leave you, MOB, needing an emotional core as strong as a military tank. If you rise to the challenge, you protect not only your own emotional health but also that of your daughter. And you *will* strive to do that because an MOB is first and foremost a mother.

Mother of the Bride, do you have it in you? The physical stamina, the nerves of steel, the emotional fortitude? Yes, you can do it—even if you have to grab a Wonder Woman cape as you blaze your daughter's trail to the altar.

And on those days when your cape begins to droop? Reach out for emotional support. If you're a woman of faith, this is the perfect time to draw strength from God. Also share your struggles with friends who can strengthen you during the rough spots on your MOB journey. It can be especially helpful to talk with those who've played the mother-of-the-bride role themselves. Let them offer the sweet balm of understanding and the benefit of wise advice.

Whatever you do to manage this role of a lifetime, Mother of the Bride, you can be proud. Remember—this gig is no job for a weakling.

A Gem for the Journey

Let your mothering skills kick in and do what you've gotta do.

Treat Yourself

Rejuvenate—pamper yourself with a facial, a massage, or a leisurely, candlelit bubble bath.

Talk It Over

Talk to your friends or sisters who have already sailed the MOB waters themselves. Ask not only for their top tips in managing your MOB challenges but also for their prayers.

A Bonus Wedding Planning Tip

Be prepared when you meet with the vendors. Research their websites and take a list of questions with you. Also make note of special requests you may have and find out if they are willing to accommodate you. (See the Wedding Vendor Worksheets at the back of the book.)

Your MOB Musings

During this demanding MOB journey, I'm drawing my strength from:

_____

_____

_____

_____

_____

_____

_____

_____

_____

_____

_____

_____

_____

_____

_____

_____

_____

Father of the Bride: Make Room for Daddy

"THIS WAS THE MOMENT I'D BEEN DREADING FOR
THE PAST SIX MONTHS. WELL, ACTUALLY FOR THE PAST
TWENTY-TWO YEARS." —GEORGE BANKS, IN THE 1991
MOVIE *FATHER OF THE BRIDE*

Father of the Bride. The title makes it sound much more appealing than it feels to the daddies who've been asked to give their little girls away. As everyone parrots the platitude "You're not losing a daughter—you're gaining a son," the father of the bride sports a smile and agrees while his heart beats a different message. One that says, "It's still going to hurt ..."

When Kristin got engaged, I wondered how Don would handle the upcoming letting go. After all, this was the man who looked through photo albums and cried when she left for college. The man who raced seventy-five miles to her rescue one night when her car broke down in a rough part of her university town. The man who wanted to fix any problem that threatened her happiness. Would he be able to walk her down the aisle and actually give her away?

As I did, Mother of the Bride, you'll have not only your own emotions to deal with but your husband's as well. He may try to appear undaunted by your daughter's impending nuptials, but on the inside an emotional wrestling match may be underway. Everything from nostalgia to worry to pride to feelings of love or loss or jealousy will tug at his heart each time his thoughts turn toward his little girl now grown.

So what can you do, MOB, to help your hubby as he transitions from being the main man in his daughter's life to being benched in favor of her new knight in shining armor?

You can start by keeping him in the loop. Be a team. If you'll rely on his listening ear and also ask for his advice, he won't feel like he's entirely out of the game. He'll still have a place of importance.

Also, in the months leading up to the wedding, think of ways to include him. Could he accompany you once to watch your sweet girl try on wedding gowns? He'd not only experience part of the fun, but the wedding would become more real to him as well. He'd see his daughter in a new light. Don got a glimpse of Kristin as a bride when he went shopping with us once while we were in Houston. Fathers of the bride *need* a practice run for this day that may hold tears.

On a more practical note, ask for your husband's help. Tour the reception site together and see what issues he may spot that you might have missed. Find out which of his friends and coworkers he'd like to include on the guest list. For an out-of-town wedding, enlist his assistance in selecting a hotel. Don contributed on this important task for both of our girls' weddings. His balanced view of the factors involved provided welcome direction and relief in the decision-making process as I tried to stay afloat in an ocean of details.

The bride-to-be can make her dad feel included by asking for his suggestions for the father-daughter dance. As they listen to various songs and practice their dance moves together, they'll create fun memories, and it will also provide Daddy with one more practice run for an emotion-laden event.

And what about cake tasting? Men love to be along for the ride when it comes time to sample food. It's amazing how their eyes glaze over when you try to discuss all the decisions that lie before you but then spring to life as soon as you mention cake tasting. In fact, MOB, if your husband is anything like Don, sampling a variety of wedding cakes will be the highlight of his wedding planning involvement.

On a more serious note, fathers of the bride actually perform a valuable service as they listen to MOBs unload the details weighing on their minds. As you discuss issues with your husband, he might provide a fresh perspective on a problem or at least an understanding ear. Don presented a few solutions that never would have occurred to me. And who knew the man had bungee cords we could use to secure tulle on pillars in desperate need of decoration? I guess you never know how your man might surprise you.

In the midst of your husband's shining moments, though, be prepared for some frustrations as well. He might resist some of your efforts to include him in the wedding-planning experience, or he may at times go into zombie mode when you need his listening ear. You may also get frustrated when he doesn't seem to care about certain decisions. And then be ready for the mother of all frustrations—the times he doesn't accomplish the one thing you ask him to do while you juggle twenty others.

I'll never forget how Don failed to pick up his tux for Kristin's wedding. Or how my brother-in-law Keith came to his rescue by scooting him out the door and down the street to the tux shop pronto. Sometimes the father of the bride needs a best man too.

After months of trying to include your husband in prenuptial activities, and after he's given you several occasions to question *your* marriage vows, the day will finally arrive, MOB, to sit back with him and watch your daughter become a "Mrs." What do you do with the father of the bride then? Rejoice with him, as together you celebrate the biggest day of your little girl's life.

Together you brought her into the world, and together you'll watch her move into a whole new world. A world, by the way, that will still include you both—though the father of the bride may have an even deeper fear about that than you do.

So remember, Mother of the Bride, don't get so immersed in wedding details that you miss helping your husband through the moment he's been dreading ever since his baby girl was born. Open your eyes—and your arms—and make room for Daddy.

A Gem for the Journey

Keep the father of the bride in the loop. Involve him in ways that will remind him he's still important.

Treat Yourself

This time, treat your man too. Go out on a date or spend the evening reminiscing over photo albums together.

Talk It Over

Ask the father of the bride what his hopes and dreams are for your daughter as she becomes a married woman. Share your dreams with him as well.

A Bonus Wedding Planning Tip

Make a list for the father of the bride of the tasks you want him to do during the wedding weekend. Include times. Help prevent forgotten duties.

Your MOB Musings

The memories closest to my heart of my little girl and her daddy are:

_____

_____

_____

_____

_____

_____

_____

_____

_____

_____

_____

_____

_____

_____

_____

_____

_____

The Man of Her Dreams Becomes Your Son: Coming to Grips with the Groom

"ACCEPT ONE ANOTHER, THEN,
JUST AS CHRIST ACCEPTED YOU ..."
—THE APOSTLE PAUL, IN ROMANS 15:7 NIV

The groom. The man of her dreams. A whole new realm to comprehend.

I've known my daughters since they first drew breath, but the men they fell in love with came to me as just that—men. No chance to figure them out as they grew up or to learn how to gauge their responses. No opportunity to study their idiosyncrasies or discover their likes and dislikes. Instead, life threw me into the deep end without a swimming lesson and expected me to come up doing the backstroke on my own.

Thank goodness Kristin and Kelli didn't present us with bad dream boyfriends. The edgiest things we had to come to grips with were motorcycles and legally owned firearms. The deep end was kind to me, and I don't take that for granted. I'm beyond grateful for the two wonderful men God brought into our girls' lives.

If you're lucky like me, Mother of the Bride, the man of your daughter's dreams will prove to be the answer to your prayers. Maybe even to years of prayers if you've prayed regularly for your daughter's future husband. Remember, when Kristin and Shawn got engaged, a new kind of joy took me by surprise as I realized we'd finally have a son. And not just any son, but a son we could be proud of and entrust our daughter to without worry. A blessing I didn't fully comprehend until it was ours.

Not everyone is as happy with their daughter's choice as we have been, though. If you fall into that category, MOB, it will require an extra measure of grace to navigate your new territory and accept the young man your daughter has chosen as your future son-in-law. You might discover that prayer can be your biggest help with such a tough assignment.

Even in the best-case scenario, mixed feelings surface from time to time. It's inevitable. A big change is underway, and big changes almost always produce a variety of emotions.

We discovered that our place in our daughters' lives diminished as soon as their boyfriends proposed. No longer did they look first to us for support and help. Their husbands-to-be now filled that role—just as they should. But that didn't make it easy. It was a change that couldn't help but hurt a little. Another step in giving them away. Joy and pain walked hand in hand once again.

Mother of the Bride, not only will you have to come to grips with the groom taking that number-one, next-of-kin spot in your daughter's life, but like me, you may also feel like he's pulling her into another family. Like you're losing her even more. You may wonder, like I did, if his family will become more important in their lives or more loved than you.

After Kristin got engaged, I struggled with knowing that Shawn's parents had a nicer home than we did and could give them more material things than we could. It hurt to see a new family shower our daughter with gifts when we wished we could be the ones to do it. I had to learn to work through those feelings and instead be happy for Kristin.

On top of feelings like these, times may arise when you're unsure of how your daughter's intended really feels about you. You may be getting along beautifully but then something happens. A comment is made, a look is noticed, or an uncomfortable silence surprises you. For whatever reason, doubt moves in momentarily, and you realize you're not as secure in your relationship with him as you are with one of your own kids. You're not as sure of his feelings.

With all this in mind, smart parents of the bride will build a solid, loving relationship with the man taking over the most important spot in their daughter's life. This process can begin at the first hint of a serious relationship and then be continued on an ongoing basis. Good relationships, no matter who's involved, take work day in and day out. If we do that work with a potential son-in-law, the result will be richer and happier lives for everyone.

How did *we* develop good relationships with our daughters' prospective grooms? We embraced them from the beginning and took advantage of every opportunity to become better acquainted. We tried to make them feel at ease and genuinely wanted.

Right away, we spent time with our girls and their guys and had fun together during their dating days. We welcomed the guys into our home and included them in some of our best-loved traditions. We introduced them to family and friends, giving them the opportunity to develop relationships within our wider circle of loved ones. We made them a part of the family before it was ever official.

We also took a genuine interest in their jobs, their dreams, their interests, and their families. We met their parents and other loved ones before the wedding and made efforts to provide the new couples with strong, unified support systems.

We also attended church together during their visits, and I began praying for my girls' guys as soon as they hit my radar. We were quick to praise Shawn's and Jake's accomplishments, and during the engagements we put them in charge of a few wedding-related tasks. We asked their opinions in their areas of expertise and even asked for their help at times. Showing excitement over their honeymoon plans and conspiring together on surprises for the girls also provided fun ways to build our bond with them.

Whether you're in the early stages of coming to grips with your daughter's groom, or well along the road to knowing and loving him, you'll benefit from using as many avenues as possible in building your relationship with your future son-in-law. If you do this, you'll truly be welcoming a son by the time the wedding day dawns.

I'll always remember the first time I saw Shawn on his and Kristin's wedding day. Members of the family and wedding party scurried around the church, completing last-minute tasks before the guests arrived. As I dashed into the sanctuary to check the flowers, I spotted Shawn talking with a couple of his groomsmen. Our eyes met. Smiles spread across our faces. The big day had finally arrived.

I reached him in seconds. The photographer captured our

hug, but what went on in my heart was known only by me. Peace and happiness welled up and overflowed. My daughter had been blessed with a wonderful man who would watch over her and care for her with faithful love.

The reception ushered in even more joy. What fun watching the newlyweds experience their first hours as husband and wife. Also, no longer were they our daughter and her intended—now they were both our kids. For the first time in our lives, we had a son.

Like us, Mother of the Bride, I hope you do far more than come to grips with your daughter's groom. I encourage you to give him your love and complete support. Let the man of her dreams become your dream come true as well.

A Gem for the Journey

Take advantage of every opportunity to build a strong relationship with the groom. You'll reap the benefits the rest of your lives.

Treat Yourself

Take the groom out, along with your husband, to one of your favorite restaurants on a day the bride is out of town or busy with other things. Bond over barbecue or steaks.

Talk It Over

Ask your future son-in-law about the people or events that have helped shape the man he is now and share likewise about your life. Ask him to share some of his favorite childhood memories.

A Bonus Wedding Planning Tip

Ask the groom to arrange for his and your daughter's transportation from the church to the reception site and also for their getaway. Boys—no matter their age—like to be in charge of the *vroom vroom.*

Your MOB Musings

I want to be a mother-in-law who:

_____

_____

_____

_____

_____

_____

_____

_____

_____

_____

_____

_____

_____

_____

_____

_____

_____

_____

11

Bye-Bye, Comfort Zone: Diving into Unfamiliar Waters

"ALL GLORY COMES FROM DARING TO BEGIN."
—WILLIAM SHAKESPEARE

Organize a wedding? Sure, I thrive on organization. Communicate with everyone? Piece of cake. I'm a writer. Communication is my business. Decorate for a party extraordinaire and create centerpieces? Now we've got a problem. I'm craft challenged and devoid of all visualization capabilities. That's right, I'll never be mistaken for Martha Stewart—or any other domestic diva for that matter.

One of the first lessons I learned as a mother of the bride is that an MOB doesn't have the luxury of operating within her comfort zone. Every MOB will have to venture outside her perimeter of confidence multiple times before the last piece of leftover wedding cake is boxed up. Yes, she'll have to dive into unfamiliar waters.

So, Mother of the Bride, saying bye-bye to your comfort

zone goes with the MOB territory. Some days you'll be called upon to fill the roles of event planner and top-notch organizer as well as financial wizard and miracle worker. Other days you'll have to morph into a professional shopper and bargain hunter, a counselor and peacekeeper, or a creative genius and craft whiz. You'll also have to play social butterfly and hostess, secretary and consummate communicator, and interviewer and mind reader. And we mustn't forget your roles as explorer and mapmaker, travel agent and personal assistant, and the ever-ready marathon runner and troubleshooter. But above all, you must present the picture of beauty and grace at all times—except when a bulldog is needed to fight for key details to your little girl's dreams, desires, and ultimate happiness.

I haven't yet met the woman who can play all these roles without, at some point, feeling like a kindergartner thrust into a college class. You, MOB, may feel either completely incompetent or totally out of place. I know I did.

Because of my deficiencies in the decorating department, tackling Hobby Lobby—the ultimate craft and home-decorating store—scared me to death the first time.

"Teri," I said to my dear friend during one of our shopping days, "would you help me look for some wedding things in Hobby Lobby?" She belonged. I didn't. Maybe if I stayed close to her, I wouldn't look as inept as I felt.

"Sure," she said. "I'd love to. What are you looking for?"

"I'm not even sure," I said as I pulled into Hobby Lobby's parking lot. "I need to choose some flowers for centerpieces and also buy some tulle, but I have no idea how much I need."

"That's okay, I'll help you figure it out."

"Actually, I have a whole list of things I need to look for." I could almost hear the store mocking me as we approached.

But with Teri by my side, I took a deep breath and braved the unknown.

I also felt out of place during some other shopping excursions. One day while scouring the city of Houston for the perfect bridal gown, Kristin and I accidentally walked into an upscale bridal shop. Within moments, the price tags alerted us to our mistake but not before a saleslady spotted us. After asking where the sale gowns were and feigning interest in a couple, we darted out the front door when no one was looking. Another time, I ventured into a high-end store searching for bridal jewelry for Kelli. I quickly discovered that some people do indeed look down their noses at regular people like me. I made a quick survey of the jewelry counter, inquired about one piece, and nearly fainted at the price. After commenting that it wouldn't work, I made a speedy exit, wishing I had worn a dressier outfit that day. I realized then that dollar bills line the boundaries of some comfort zones.

Of course, meeting with florists also challenged my feelings of intelligence and domestic self-worth. I didn't know a begonia from a peony. It's a good thing mothers of the bride aren't disqualified from service for floral infractions, or my poor girls would have been planning their weddings minus their momma.

By now it should come as no surprise that the decorating day before each of my daughters' weddings loomed large for me. The demands of the day made me want to call in sick. But, alas, the mother of the bride can't do that. I just went as prepared as possible and gave orders to the bridal troops—otherwise known as bridesmaids and family members—and then depended on their superior abilities to help make our decorating dreams a reality.

Of course, the chaos that accompanied such a large operation of volunteers put a major strain on my super-organized psyche. While some bombarded me with questions, others rifled through my carefully labeled boxes and carried things off to parts unknown. With my comfort zone nowhere in sight, I soldiered on, hanging on to the promise of the rehearsal dinner—the one place where I had no responsibility. A place MOBs like to call heaven.

To balance out the rehearsal dinner taste of heaven, the dreaded salon experience awaited me on my girls' wedding days. Since I never get my hair styled or colored and only go to my small-town salon for haircuts, I might as well have been wearing a neon sign that blinked *hick from the sticks* when the time came to get my hair done at the high-class salons Kristin and Kelli selected. No one forced me to go. It was my choice. I didn't want the hassle of fixing my own hair for the big events, so instead I braved the fancy salons and new stylists. Unfortunately, neither experience was pleasant, as it took a couple of tries to get the stylists to fix my hair the way I requested. Thank goodness the end results didn't hint at the earlier turmoil.

Finally, meeting and socializing with new people, especially our daughters' future in-laws, thrust me into uncomfortable territory. It's no wonder nerves came along for the ride when the blending of two families hung in the balance. Since we met our girls' in-laws for the first time in restaurants, at least we avoided the additional pressure of presenting our homes in a good light. We didn't plan it that way for that reason, but it did help reduce the stress. And reduced stress gets high marks in any MOB's book.

As mothers of the bride—and as women in general—each time we square our shoulders and say good-bye to our comfort zones, it leads to growth and more self-confidence. By the time

Jake proposed to Kelli, Hobby Lobby felt like a home away from home. Not because I had become handy at crafts, but because I knew that store like my own kitchen by the time Kristin's wedding had come and gone. I even bought fabric on my own the second time around—though I did fear at any moment being exposed as a seamstress imposter.

While planning Kelli's wedding, I also felt more confident when meeting with the florist and other vendors. Even on the dreaded decorating day, I knew I'd face a steady diet of curveballs, but at least I had mentally prepared for them. And when it came time to hostess the wedding reception, I put on a smile and made my way from table to table, even introducing myself to folks from Jake's side of the guest list. I still haven't conquered my fear of salons or high-end boutiques, but I suppose that gives me something to shoot for in the future.

So where are you on your journey, MOB? Have you had to dive into unfamiliar waters yet? If not, don't be surprised if they're just around the bend. Take courage from my fledgling efforts, then square your shoulders, take a deep breath, and make your baby's dreams come true. You'll be catching curveballs in no time.

A Gem for the Journey

Ask a friend to join you as you venture out of your comfort zone. The Bible tells us two are better than one.

Treat Yourself

Take a break from new territory and curl up on the sofa with a cup of your favorite tea.

Talk It Over

Confide in a friend or relative about any insecurities or fears that you're dealing with as a mother of the bride. Listen to your confidante's encouraging words and take them to heart.

A Bonus Wedding Planning Tip

To help you make your final shopping decisions, take photos of fabric, flowers, ribbon, and other décor so you can remember which items you saw at various stores. You can even do this when shopping for the bridal gown and bridesmaids' dresses unless it's prohibited at certain shops. Also ask sales personnel if fabric samples are available.

Your MOB Musings

As a mother of the bride, I've had to leave my comfort zone behind when:

_____

_____

_____

_____

_____

_____

_____

_____

_____

_____

_____

_____

_____

_____

_____

_____

Lean on Me:
The MOB's Support Team

"WHAT DO WE LIVE FOR, IF NOT TO MAKE THE WORLD
LESS DIFFICULT FOR EACH OTHER?" —GEORGE ELIOT

At the beginning of every bridal journey, a billboard should proclaim, "Warning to Brides and Their Mothers: Never Attempt to Handle an Entire Wedding on Your Own." How true. Brides and moms need help and lots of it. Some have wedding planners to manage all the details and calm them when things get stressful. Like many others, we had friends and family.

Granted, those able to hire wedding coordinators are as lucky as lottery winners, but they number in the minority. If you're like me, Mother of the Bride, you'll need a team of volunteers. I discovered that raising a child—or at least a daughter—isn't the only thing that takes a village. Getting her to a state of wedded bliss calls for a small army as well.

It's never too early to compile your list of potential MOB supporters. As you do, keep in mind that many will play minor roles, helping only with a task or two. You'll need lots of these the weekend of the wedding. They'll do everything from transporting flowers from the church to the reception site to carrying gifts to the designated vehicle after the bride and groom make their getaway. At this point, only the most loyal remain to help you pack up the wedding wonderland you've worked so hard to create.

Long before this weekend arrives, however, you'll need to call on the heavy lifters: the ones you'll ask for bigger favors, for deeper investments of time and energy. Ones otherwise known as your closest family and friends.

If you have more than one daughter, MOB, you'll witness firsthand how a wedding causes the sisterly bond to surface and thrive, even when they live hours apart like my girls did. During the months of planning Kelli's wedding, Kristin joined us for a bridal gown shopping day, traveled again to help hostess the shower, and provided lots of long-distance help. Among other things, she became our Hobby Lobby backup when stores in our area were out of certain items. She also sent shower invitations, did online research, and e-mailed the wedding weekend itinerary to all the major players as well as the entire family. She and Shawn even put together a professional-quality slide show for the reception.

My own sisters also supplied help during my days as an MOB. They offered emotional support from afar as I e-mailed them weekly, unloading tales of my crazy schedule and the latest problems I'd had to troubleshoot. However, when our daughters' wedding weekends arrived, the sisters' support shifted to hands-on help. Help that was much needed and deeply appreciated by this hanging-on-by-her-fingertips mother of the bride.

Since my sister Carolyn lives in Tulsa, where Kristin's wedding took place, she got sucked into the eye of the bridal storm on a few other occasions as well. My calls to her went something like this:

"Carolyn, when we have Kristin's bridal portrait taken, could we leave her dress in your office while we run errands and get her hair done?" Then a few days later, "Would you mind picking up Kristin's dress at the cleaners for me?" Next, the biggie, "Would it be okay if the whole family gathers at your house while they're in town for the wedding? And, would you mind shopping for the groceries if I give you some money?"

Even though Kelli got married in a different city, I still called on Carolyn. "Would you help me select a mat and frame at Michael's for Kelli's bridal portrait? Could you pick it up and bring it with you the weekend of the wedding?" I guess that's what happens when you're the sister who lives nearest the MOB.

When it comes to a listening ear, the best friend and the closest family members will undoubtedly split the role. Every time I called my mom, she got an earful of wedding. Don, of course, got regular updates—though he heard the abbreviated version so we could avoid the glazed-over eyes that afflict most fathers of the bride. The details flowed, however, to my friend Teri and also to Kristin during Kelli's wedding prep. They understood that I got a measure of relief by simply telling someone I had to make another out-of-town Hobby Lobby run or by filling them in on the latest chapter of the invitation saga. In fact, I might have lost my sanity if it weren't for them.

And speaking of sanity savers, MOB, chances are you'll find yourself calling on one member of your support team more than any other. She will become your right-hand man—or more accurately, your right-hand woman. She may be your sister, your daughter, or your best friend. Whatever the relationship, she'll be with you from your initial squeals of excitement all the way through till the toasts and the dancing.

My dear friend Teri served as my right-hand woman for both of my daughters' weddings. Without her presence and Martha Stewart abilities, I would never have had the courage to walk into Hobby Lobby the first time, let alone purchase fabric on my own one day.

Teri did everything from being my Hobby Lobby partner to helping me shop for my dress to making garters for my girls. She created Kristin's candle-ring centerpieces, a gorgeous floral arrangement, and Kelli's wedding-cake card box. She even enlisted her daughter's help when we needed additional expertise. She helped me hostess bridal showers for both girls and also agreed to be my eyes and ears at Kelli's reception until I could get there. She hung tough with me during all-day shopping expeditions and understood when I was too overwhelmed to think clearly. Yes, she was an MOB sanity saver.

The only person trumping Teri in the sanity-saving department was God himself. He's my strong support in all areas of life, wedding planning included. He cares about everything that concerns me. He is the ultimate listening ear. I can talk to him about anything and say, "Here it is, Lord. I need your help." And he does it. He helps me.

So, Mother of the Bride, when wedding planning towers over you and when your friends, family, and God all say, "Why don't you let me help? Why don't you lean on me?" go ahead and accept their help. Go ahead and lean on them. Before you know it, you'll be paying it forward. One day *you'll* be the listening ear for another frazzled MOB. One day you'll get to make the world less difficult for someone else. ◯

A Gem for the Journey

Share the excitement of being behind the scenes. Don't be afraid to ask for help. You need it, and others enjoy playing a role.

Treat Yourself

Next time you're on an MOB mission with someone from your support team, take time to stop at a spot you both love—a favorite bookstore, coffee shop, or ice cream parlor. Relax and refresh yourselves!

Talk It Over

Meditate on the following verse from the Bible and then ask God to help you in your areas of need:

"For I am the Lord your God who takes hold of your right hand and says to you, Do not fear; I will help you" (Isaiah 41:13 NIV).

A Bonus Wedding Planning Tip

Plan wedding weekend assignments for members of the bridal party as well as family members. Who will take the guestbook from the church to the reception site? Who will carry the candelabras to which vehicle after the ceremony? Who will be in charge of the gifts after the reception? Write all assignments down and hand them out at the rehearsal.

Your MOB Musings

The people I can ask to be part of my support team are:

_____

_____

_____

_____

_____

_____

_____

_____

_____

_____

_____

_____

_____

_____

_____

_____

_____

_____

Just Because You Love Her: Going Above and Beyond

"Mom, you're never going to believe this," Kristin said.

My head jerked to attention. Those are words a parent never wants to hear, especially in a call from six hundred miles away.

"What's going on?" I asked.

"Well ... the invitations arrived, and there's a mistake on them," she said, her tone dead serious.

"You're kidding. What did they do?"

"The name of the reception hall is misspelled."

"Oh, good grief," I said. "I guess I'll have to call them. They're going to have to fix it—and for no extra charge," I continued, pronouncing judgment and solution in rapid-fire succession.

"But, Mom, here's the problem. We're the ones who made the mistake." My heart dropped. Dread replaced my initial irritation.

"Oh no. Are you sure?"

"Yes, I checked my copy of our order form. Pull yours out and you'll see what I mean." I grabbed my folder, flipping through paperwork while she went on. "I can't believe I made a mistake. I'm so sorry, Mom. I feel just sick about it."

That's when I saw it. With evidence of our error now glaring before me, I inwardly groaned, accepted the fact, then tried to ease her distress. "Kristin, we both missed it. I checked it over before you sent it in. Our eyes must have skimmed right over the name of the reception hall since we're so familiar with it. Don't worry, though. We'll get it fixed."

She protested, knowing it would add to an already long list of expenses, but I assured her we would not send out invitations with mistakes on them. Since the problem involved the name of the reception site, not only would guests key in on it, but it might also cause confusion since many were coming from out of town. More than that, it would mar one of Kristin and Shawn's wedding keepsakes.

Some would argue—and did—that having the invitations redone was unnecessary. They said people wouldn't care. But I cared. And I knew Kristin and Shawn cared, even though they would never demand or even ask to have the invitations reprinted. It all boiled down to love. We loved our daughter and wanted the best for her. We wanted to spare her from any embarrassment, and we also wanted her to have a perfect invitation keepsake. We would go to the extra expense just because we loved her.

Mother of the Bride, you'll have your own opportunities to go above and beyond for your daughter. Hopefully you won't face wedding invitation woes, but other issues will undoubtedly present themselves. It goes with the territory. More people may RSVP yes than you ever imagined, your daughter's wedding gown may be more expensive than you hoped, you may miscount and need to order several dozen more truffles or chocolate-covered strawberries for the guest tables. As the runaway wedding train gathers steam, your first impulse might be a spending freeze. Instead, view it as an opportunity to show an extra measure of love and consideration for your precious bride-to-be. Go above and beyond.

Of course, you must also be prudent when going above and beyond. Don't get carried away with this idea and drain your bank account in an effort to show your daughter how much you love her. Instead, anticipate a few extra expenses and build them into your budget.

If mishaps don't open the door for bestowing extravagant love, you can still do nice things for your daughter. I bought bridal planners and magazines for my girls, treated Kelli to professional manicures for her bridal portrait session and her wedding day, hosted a bridal reunion-luncheon for Kristin and her bridesmaids, and also found special gifts for each couple to serve as mementos of a memorable detail of their own wedding experience.

Other just-because-you-love-her gestures could include sending her a sweet or funny card, surprising her with a little luxury item not in her budget, giving her a girly bridal shower to remember, whisking her away for an impromptu brunch or dessert, or even making a deeper financial sacrifice on an aspect of the wedding especially important to her. You know better than anyone else what will make your daughter smile. Go for it. Find ways during this unique time of her life to show her how much she means to you.

Keep in mind that going above and beyond doesn't have to be limited to things you buy or do. It can also encompass qualities as well. Be pleasant. Be fun! Strive to be unselfish, forgiving, and wise in what you say and don't say. Love your daughter's intended and accept her new in-laws. Be supportive and always ready to provide a listening ear. In short, do your best to be a loving and helpful mother of the bride.

Before you know it, the wedding day will arrive—along with your chance for a final "above and beyond" before your little girl becomes a Mrs., before her main support system officially changes. What's the best thing you can do for her, MOB, as she pledges her life to another? Let her go. Allow her and her beloved to become their own family. Don't interfere in their lives. If that sounds too final, take heart. She'll still be your little girl. That will never change. Take it from me, it *is* possible to stay involved and supportive without crossing the line into meddling.

The entire wedding-planning experience will afford countless opportunities to lavish extra love on your precious daughter. Take advantage of each one. Your giving spirit and loving actions will proclaim the depth of your feelings for her when words fall short. Much like Christ's sacrificial love for us, his children, your willingness to sacrifice for your daughter will never be forgotten.

So, Mother of the Bride, gather your energy—and your pocketbook—and go above and beyond. Just because you love her.

A Gem for the Journey

These are once-in-a-lifetime days. Show your love at every opportunity.

Treat Yourself

Splurge on a fun outing with the bride-to-be. Attend a concert, go to a movie, or try a new restaurant. You'll both be blessed!

Talk It Over

Watch for an opportunity to tell your daughter how much you love her. Share with her the moments you will journal about today in Your MOB Musings.

A Bonus Wedding Planning Tip

Make copies of all agreements and orders with vendors and keep all wedding expense receipts together in case there is a miscommunication or need to return something.

Your MOB Musings

Some of the moments when my love for my daughter has filled my heart to overflowing include:

_____

_____

_____

_____

_____

_____

_____

_____

_____

_____

_____

_____

_____

_____

_____

_____

_____

Life Goes On Too?
It's Not All about the Wedding

"WE ARE HARD PRESSED ON EVERY SIDE ..."
—THE APOSTLE PAUL, IN 2 CORINTHIANS 4:8 NIV

"Cheryl, this is Kim out at Asbury Village," I heard after answering the phone on Memorial Day afternoon. "I'm worried about Frances. When I got here, the day shift told me she's been sick all day. She's nauseated and even a little swollen."

"She is? I wonder why someone didn't call us earlier." Kim and I both knew this didn't bode well, given my mother-in-law's complex medical problems.

"I don't know. But I've called the nurse. She's off because of the holiday, but she suggested that you and Don come check on Frances and see if you think she needs to go to the ER."

"Okay. We'll be there in a few minutes. Thanks for calling."

And thus began another health crisis and hospital stay for Don's mother. Since Kelli's wedding was fewer than seven weeks away, the onset of this ordeal discouraged me even more than usual.

From previous experience, I knew we might face several weeks of increased stress. Events soon confirmed my fears. In fact, this crisis proved to be even more serious than others had been.

To complicate matters, in just two days Don would start summer school, the most demanding month on his teaching calendar. Also, the next day was a huge day for me as an MOB. I was scheduled to join Kelli in Missouri for her bridal portrait session. Thank goodness, Don had one free day left and could be with his mom. Not only did I *want* to be with Kelli for this special day, but I had her wedding gown. I *had* to be there.

So off I drove the next morning with Kelli's bridal attire filling the backseat. I put worries of what the future might hold out of mind and delighted in the prospect of spending a memorable day with my baby-turned-bride.

Relief that I was able to come flashed across both our faces as we greeted one another. We needed this day to work. We didn't have any wiggle room. We wanted to display Kelli's bridal portrait at the reception. If we cancelled the session, it would have been impossible to secure our location again and reschedule the photographer before it was too late. As one thing after another fell beautifully into place, we felt beyond thankful.

Back at home the next day, however, reality came calling. Mom's situation was serious. Within days, her condition grew even more grim. She had to be transferred to a hospital in another city. Now I would be traveling daily on top of everything else. I felt as if I was drowning.

As Don and I drove home that first evening, I finally cracked under the pressure. I got angry. I cried. I told Don I didn't want to do it. I didn't want to be the one to shoulder the responsibility. He had no easy answers, though, because there were none. I would just have to do it. I grew quiet, but inwardly the struggle raged on. I cried out to God, pouring out my frustration, but I also asked for his help and the strength to deal with each issue I faced. I knew I could rest in him. He would carry me through.

Since wedding tasks awaited me in yet another city, Don's sister Susie drove nearly three hours to be with her mom so I could have a day off hospital duty. Unfortunately, that day off included traveling again and a massive to-do list, but at least I got to take care of business.

I could go on with the saga, but I won't. Suffice it to say that in the midst of demanding wedding preparations, life had the audacity to go on as well—as it does for every mother of the bride. If it hasn't happened to you yet, MOB, I'm sure it soon will. As a mother of the bride, you may not have time for insurance problems or car repairs, and you certainly don't have time to get sick. Sadly, however, such normal-life headaches don't stop because you're planning the event of a lifetime. Somehow the world doesn't get the memo to revolve around your wedding-planning schedule now.

So be prepared. Work deadlines will still loom. Bills will still need to be paid, and laundry will still pile up. Grocery shopping, cleaning, errands, church or club obligations, and other regular duties will continue to cry out for attention. Other stuff of life will come up as well. Funerals, weddings, doctor appointments, holidays, special events for family and friends, caregiving responsibilities, maintaining friendships, and even the occasional haircut. That's right. Your hair doesn't quit growing just because you're a mother of the bride.

Not only will all these things happen, but you'll also still need to be a wife to your husband and a mom to your other kids. While I helped plan Kristin's wedding, Kelli had major events going on in her life as well. To finish her college degree, she had to complete an internship in Houston. She needed help moving, getting settled, and then moving back before graduation. In the midst of all this, she also endured some rocky times with her then-boyfriend. In other words, she still needed her mom. And since I wanted to stand by her just as badly as I wanted to help our bride-to-be Kristin, I reached down and pulled up my mom bootstraps and gave her the support she needed.

So how does a mother of the bride handle it when life goes on right in the middle of wedding preparations? As for me, I trimmed back where I could. I said no when asked to take on extra responsibilities, I didn't attend certain events, and I chose not to sign up for a favorite mission trip. I also asked for occasional help with some of my commitments and even granted myself grace at home by doing some of my chores on a more relaxed schedule.

I put another sanity-saving strategy into practice as well. I took things one step at a time. Or at least I tried to. Instead of constantly envisioning all the tasks before me, I focused on one or two challenges at a time. Of course, I had to keep the big picture in mind, too, but I didn't allow myself to think in those terms all the time. It was too overwhelming. Instead, I remembered that wedding planning is a marathon, and I paced myself accordingly.

Finally, I comforted myself with the knowledge that life would slow down again one day. Surely our schedules could never be any busier than they currently were. The year Kristin got married, not only did Kelli graduate from college the week before Kristin's wedding, but Kristin graduated with her master's degree the week prior to Kelli's graduation. And all of these events took place in different states—none of which was *our* state.

When I told people about the crazy month we were facing, I'd say, "If I can just make it through May, I'll be okay. I'll collapse after that." Little did I know, those words would prove to be prophetic. I took a fall on June 1 and broke a rib. I *had* to slow down then. Pain prevented me from doing anything at more than a snail's pace. But hey, at least I made it through May, right?

So, Mother of the Bride, trim back where you can, take it a step at a time, and look forward to slowing down after the wedding. Just try not to break any ribs. And remember, as you plan your little girl's big day, expect life to go on. After all, it's not all about the wedding.

A Gem for the Journey

Be prepared. Have some sanity-saving strategies in place to help you deal with life's daily demands as you wade through wedding planning.

Treat Yourself

Lighten your load. Arrange for someone else to take over at least one of your responsibilities for a while.

Talk It Over

Spend some time talking with your other kids. In casual conversation, find out what their biggest concerns are right now. Also talk about the happy things going on in their lives and rejoice with them.

A Bonus Wedding Planning Tip

To ensure that your daughter's bridal portrait will be finished and framed by the wedding weekend, have any needed alterations to the bridal gown completed at least two months prior to the wedding—and earlier if possible. Try to schedule the portrait session no later than the two-month mark. Also, watch for sales and use coupons when purchasing a frame and other décor. If you're on a very tight budget, you can often cut costs in half with coupons and sales. Don't forget to check clearance aisles as well.

Your MOB Musings

Sometimes I feel like I'm being pushed beyond my limits, and in those moments I:

_____

_____

_____

_____

_____

_____

_____

_____

_____

_____

_____

_____

_____

_____

_____

_____

15

Be Very Careful: No Do-Overs for the MOB

"TREAD SOFTLY BECAUSE YOU TREAD ON MY DREAMS."
—WILLIAM BUTLER YEATS

We've all been there; we've all had moments we regret, moments we wish we could do over. At times that's possible. Some situations, like various tasks or games, lend themselves quite well to do-overs. However, when relationships and feelings are involved, that's another matter. Even if we get a second chance, the memory of the original situation will never be entirely wiped out.

What does this mean for you, Mother of the Bride? It means *be very careful*. You get only one shot at certain things. You can't redo your first response to the news of your daughter's engagement or your initial reaction to her ring. You can't go back and relive wedding day moments that will never happen again. You've got to be one step ahead at all times—ready to keep a negative or lackluster response in check, ready to fully live the fleeting moments that will never come your way again.

Remember my story in chapter 2 about the first time I saw Kristin's ring? I had just driven ten hours, and my reaction lacked the unbridled emotion the moment called for. I sure wish I'd been able to match her excitement level that evening. I did my best, though, to make up for it the next day with one of my signature squeals.

Other MOB wish-I-could-do-it-over moments can be impossible to correct. One of my biggest failures happened during the moments preceding Kristin's wedding. I'd been busy—like any mother of the bride—helping the bride get ready, making sure everyone and everything was in place, and greeting our guests. Before I knew it, it was time to line up for the processional. Nervous about walking down the aisle at the right time, I failed to go back and have a few special words with my daughter.

Oh, how I wish I could reclaim those moments. I would tell her how beautiful she looked and how much I loved her. You can bet that at Kelli's wedding a few years later, I made sure not to miss such a moment with her. If you, Mother of the Bride, happen to fail in some way during one of those moments you can't recapture, try looking for a way to redeem the mistake. For example, I could have sent Kristin a beautiful card after the wedding with a handwritten note telling her the things I wished I'd said. I could have transformed the loss into a treasure of a different sort.

Some of our blunders as mothers of the bride cut a little deeper than a missed opportunity or failure to show proper enthusiasm, though. When it comes to careless words or criticism, we can attempt to rectify the situation with apologies or explanations, but hurtful words, once they're spoken, are difficult to erase. Even with backpedaling or forgiveness asked and received, a root of insecurity may linger—not to mention an unhappy memory.

These unfortunate moments might come in the form of critical remarks about choices the bride and groom make. Kelli and Jake chose a very simple wedding invitation that ended up looking quite elegant. Before I saw the finished product and knew they'd definitely made the right choice, I voiced some reservations. I feared we might be perceived as unwilling to spring for something nicer. I realize now that it was my worry and not their choice that was the problem. Even though I didn't speak in an unkind way, my comments may have hurt Kelli's feelings or at the very least caused her unnecessary stress. Now I wish I had kept my opinion to myself.

Another moment you might want to do over, MOB, could happen when you're particularly stressed and mutter a complaint about the work or expense involved with the wedding. Unless it's said in a lighthearted way, be sure to voice your frustrations to someone other than the bride or groom. That's when your closest confidantes come in handy. And always remember to avoid statements like, "If my name is going to be on the invitation, then ..." or "If we're paying for this wedding, then ..." Be careful, MOB. Don't steal the happy couple's joy before the big day ever arrives.

The wish-I-could-do-it-over list also includes critical or unkind remarks about the groom or his family. You may have good reason for your observations, Mother of the Bride, but voicing them to your daughter will put her in an awkward or defensive position. You might even undermine the good relationships she needs to form. The psalmist David said, "Set a guard over my mouth, Lord; keep watch over the door of my lips" (Psalm 141:3 NIV). So, MOB, guard your words, or you may wind up eating a slice of regret instead of cake at the wedding party.

Sometimes unhappy moments can unfold when you forget to be sensitive to the bride's stresses and emotions. I'll never forget reprimanding Kristin at the end of a long and less-than-successful shopping day. Tired and discouraged, she refused to do a simple task that would have eased my load. I thought she deserved some straight talk from her mom, but it pushed her past her limit, causing her to cry. It wasn't worth it, and I regret it to this day.

Other times, moments you might like to do over happen if you and your daughter have very different styles of accomplishing tasks. Kelli and I had trouble settling into a good working relationship during wedding planning. She wanted to do one task at a time without thinking about another. I felt it important to give attention to several issues at once before time grew short and wedding chores piled up.

After several episodes of unhappy communication and hurt feelings on both our parts, Kelli and I spoke plainly about the problem, cried together, and agreed to be more sensitive to each other's feelings and work styles. That honest discussion vastly improved our wedding-planning relationship.

Mother of the Bride, if you and your daughter are having communication problems, try initiating a conversation where you can be completely honest with one another. You'll each discover ways to be more thoughtful of the other. And if you share your needs, wants, and expectations in the early stages of working together, you might be able to avoid problems later on.

Good relationships and happy memories need careful nurturing during all phases of life, wedding planning included. As a mother of the bride, tread softly while preparing for the most important day of your daughter's life. Remember, do-overs rarely exist for the MOB. Do your best to get it right the first time—and give yourself grace when you don't. After all, apologies and forgiveness go a long way toward healing mistakes.

A Gem for the Journey

Enjoy special moments fully and guard your words and reactions at all times.

Treat Yourself

De-stress by playing a computer or video game. You can do it over as many times as you like!

Talk It Over

Tell your daughter you're sorry for any mistakes you've made where she's concerned, whether during wedding planning or at other times. Ask for her forgiveness and then go forward together with fresh joy.

A Bonus Wedding Planning Tip

Arrange for someone else to pin the corsages and boutonnieres and prepare the flower girl's rose petals before the ceremony so you can catch a few extra moments with the bride.

Your MOB Musings

Some of the things so far that I wish I could do over as an MOB and some possible remedies are:

_____

_____

_____

_____

_____

_____

_____

_____

_____

_____

_____

_____

_____

_____

_____

_____

When Dreams Become Disasters: The Dreaded Horror Stories

"YIELD NOT TO CALAMITY, BUT FACE HER BOLDLY."
—VIRGIL

"What a nightmare," I said to Don after the second attempt at having Kristin's bridal gown cleaned in the weeks following her bridal portrait session. "They put *new* spots on the dress. I don't know what I'm going to do."

Talk about a horror story. Most weddings have at least one. The caterer goes out of business right before the wedding. The bridesmaids' dresses arrive at the last minute—in the wrong color. The unthinkable wedding cake mishap actually happens. And now, Mother of the Bride, you may have a woeful account of your own brewing.

So what do you do when the fairy-tale wedding you're helping your daughter orchestrate no longer feels so happily ever after—when part of the dream has become a disaster before your very eyes? Do you face the ordeal, determined to see it finally result in delight, or do you allow the wedding-planning roller coaster to plunge you into despair?

Maybe one of my horror stories could give you courage for yours. Kristin's bridal gown story could actually be described as a trilogy. That's right, a horror story trilogy.

The saga began with our quest to acquire Kristin's dream gown. She fell in love right away with one we found at a nationwide chain featuring beautiful off-the-rack gowns. Trouble started, however, when it came time to make the purchase.

"We'd like to get this gown," I said to the shop manager, "but would you please order a new one for us? This one is damaged."

"We can order the gown from another one of our stores," she said, "but we can't order a brand-new one from the factory. Also, you'll have to pay in full when you place your order."

"But if you order from another store, that gown might be damaged, too, if it's been tried on multiple times."

"Well, that's our policy. Remember, we have an alterations department that can make repairs."

About to lose my cool, I said, "We don't *want* to buy a gown that needs repairs. And with your 'all sales final' policy, you're asking me to take a risk on a very large purchase—a risk that a different off-the-rack gown will be in excellent condition."

She shrugged her shoulders. "I'm sorry, but that's our policy."

"Then it's an unreasonable policy." I sighed and then paused for a moment. "I'd like to get this dress for my daughter, but I can't do it under these terms."

We left the store with our high-flying bridal-shopping spirits dashed to the ground. Kristin struggled to hold back tears, and I felt awful. I had failed my baby girl. I had not ordered the dress she wanted. She understood the reasons, but it still hurt.

Unwilling to give up, I said, "Let's go check their other shops here in the Houston area. Maybe we can find another one in your size and in good condition. We'd be able to see it rather than order one sight unseen."

Kristin readily agreed to my plan, and for the next couple of days we tramped all over the greater metropolitan area but to no avail. She would not be able to get her dream gown. I convinced her to look at other dresses, but her heart wasn't in it. She compared each one to the dress she loved, and nothing measured up.

When it was time for me to head home, a cloud of disappointment hung over us. As I made the trek northward, my mind flitted from one wedding concern to another. A few hours into the trip, I got a call from the bride-to-be. Hope was on the horizon.

Kristin had told Sarah, one of her bridesmaids, about the dress ordeal. Sarah couldn't believe it. She called the bridal store's Tulsa location and got an entirely different story. They would be happy to order a brand-new dress for us.

Kristin's voice bubbled with sheer joy, and I hooted in victory. I could make my little girl's dream come true after all. The bridal gown horror story had just turned into a fairy tale.

Unfortunately, fairy tales always harbor a villain, and two months before the wedding, another villain threatened our happily-ever-after ending. Two villains, in fact—the two incompetent dry-cleaning establishments we dealt with after Kristin's bridal portrait.

The thought of a bridal portrait session made me nervous from the beginning. I feared the problems we might encounter getting the gown clean after its foray into a non-carpeted world. My worst fears, however, didn't come close to the nightmare that unfolded.

Since our small town had only one dry-cleaning establishment and since the bridal portrait session would take place in Tulsa, we decided to get the gown cleaned there. Shawn even offered to get a recommendation from the Tulsa bridal shop where his sisters bought their wedding gowns.

The portrait session went beautifully, but the dress did indeed get dirty. Afterward, when we arrived at the recommended dry cleaners, Kristin and I noticed it looked run down. We also spotted two little dogs running free in the shop. We looked at each other and grimaced but went ahead and showed the manager the soiled areas on the gown and left it with them. While walking to the car, we voiced our concerns, but since the business had been referred to us by a reputable and elegant bridal shop, we trusted all would be well. What a mistake that turned out to be.

Several days later, I drove back to pick up the gown. Before paying the bill, I checked the dress. It wasn't clean. Frustrated, I pointed out several places that still needed attention and then arranged for my sister Carolyn to pick up the gown for me. She could bring it to our home when she came for Kristin's bridal shower that weekend.

A couple of days later, Carolyn called with bad news. "Cheryl, the dry cleaners still didn't get the dress clean. I didn't want to pick it up without checking with you."

"Oh, no," I said. "I can't believe this is happening."

"I know. I don't feel very good about this place. It smelled like smoke, and those dogs you mentioned were still running around."

"Oh, good grief. I wish we'd never left the dress there. I'm not sure what to do."

I thanked her for her help and then discussed the situation with Kristin. We decided it was time to rescue the dress. We didn't want it in that store a second longer than necessary.

Since Shawn and his mom would be driving through Tulsa on their way to the shower, we put them on rescue duty. Their marching orders? Express our dissatisfaction, refuse to pay the bill for a still-dirty gown, and then get it the heck out of there—all without Shawn, the groom, actually seeing the dress.

That Saturday they arrived at our house with dress in hand, their mission a success. I, however, still had a huge problem—a bridal gown that was not only dirty but also now littered with dog hairs and smelled bad. Things couldn't get any worse.

After some thought, I decided to give our local dry cleaners a try. I explained our predicament, showed them the problem areas, and then begged them to tell me up front if they didn't think they could get it clean. They assured me they could do it. I left the gown with them and crossed my fingers.

I wish I could say they solved my problem, but remember, this *is* a horror story. Not only did they not get the dress clean, but new spots appeared as well. They tried to convince me that no one would notice. With as much control as I could muster, I said, "I want my daughter's wedding gown in pristine condition when she walks down the aisle. I'll have to take it elsewhere."

With worry now in full bloom and prayers for God's help intensifying with each passing day, I called the bridal shop where we bought the dress, relayed our nightmare, and asked for their best recommendation for a dry cleaner. The manager answered with calm assurance. "We always recommend Yale Cleaners. They do an excellent job."

Once again I headed to Tulsa. The young woman at Yale Cleaners, which by its very appearance inspired confidence, told me they could take care of the dress. And miracle of miracles, they did. Not only did they restore the gown to its spotless beauty, they restored my sanity as well. I gushed my gratitude and positively floated home.

From that point on, I went into protection mode. As instructed, I hung the gown with the train fully extended. I also wrapped clean sheets around it to protect it from dust and other unthinkable accidents. Anyone approaching would have to go through me first. I was like a momma bear guarding her cubs.

Now that the gown was gorgeous again, our fairy tale appeared to be back on track. Unbeknownst to us, however, the third chapter of our horror story still lay before us.

Just days before the wedding, we decided Kristin should try the gown on with her bridal jewelry in case the necklace needed to be shortened. After helping her into the dress, I turned her toward the bedroom mirror, ready to ooh and ahh over what we saw. Instead, we looked at each other in shock. The dress was too long.

How was this possible? How could it be longer now than before it was cleaned? A few years later we learned that the fabric had probably been stretched during the cleaning and steaming process, but at this point, we panicked. We had no time for alterations. The fairy tale had once again turned horror story.

In desperation, I tried to build Kristin's shoes up with heel pads I already had. Not only did the pads look ridiculous with her beautiful satin sandals, but they also didn't work. They hurt her feet and made her wobble.

Growing ever more frantic, we thought of a petticoat. Maybe it would take up the extra length. Kristin thought Shawn's sister might still have hers, so I made an emergency call to his mom. They did indeed have the petticoat. Linda said they'd bring it to the bridesmaids' luncheon in Tulsa, now just two days away. We breathed a sigh of relief but would not rest easy until Kristin tried on the petticoat with the dress.

As soon as the luncheon was over, we hurried to Carolyn's house. Kristin could try the gown on there. We crossed our fingers, held our breath, and prayed. The petticoat worked! It provided just enough bulk to take up the extra length. The wedding gown of her dreams was once again restored, and the last chapter of our horror story trilogy had come to an end.

And you know what? When Kristin walked down the aisle on her wedding day, all memories of our wedding gown woes melted away. Nothing took away from our joy in that moment. All we saw was a breathtakingly beautiful bride, glowing in loveliness and grace, a bashful blush to her cheeks, and eyes only for her groom. A true fairy-tale scene.

Will you have a horror story unfold as you prepare for your daughter's wedding, MOB? Hopefully not, but chances are something major will go wrong at some point. When it does, don't let disaster dampen your joy. Remember my horror story trilogy and take heart. Problems can be solved, and God does intervene.

A Gem for the Journey

Determine to hang on through a disaster. The delight will come.

Treat Yourself

Call in the disaster relief team. Tell your sisters and girlfriends you need some pampering and let them swoop in and do their magic in whatever way they choose.

Talk It Over

Call or have coffee with your mom, your sister, or your best friend and tell her your wedding-planning horror stories in all their excruciating detail. Downplay the events with the bride, however, and try to shield her from unnecessary stress.

A Bonus Wedding Planning Tip

Ask your dry cleaner which method they use to remove wrinkles from bridal gowns. Steaming is preferable since physical contact is not made with the fabric, but stubborn wrinkles or pleats may require hand pressing. Ask them to keep pressing to a minimum so stretching won't occur.

Your MOB Musings

My wedding planning horror stories and how I dealt with them happened when:

_____

_____

_____

_____

_____

_____

_____

_____

_____

_____

_____

_____

_____

_____

_____

_____

_____

17

The MOB Dress:
Time to Splurge on You

The day has finally come, Mother of the Bride. Now that all the major details of the wedding are well underway, it's time to focus on you. Time to shop for the all-important MOB dress. Time to splurge on *you*.

At this stage of wedding planning, your pocketbook may stage a revolt, but I give you permission to fight back. After all, you're the mother of the bride—the second most important woman at the wedding. You need to shine too.

As you finally begin thinking about your dress instead of the bridal gown, you might inwardly proclaim: *Finally, it's all about me. This time, I'm the one who gets to choose!*

Well, dear MOB, you're almost right. When you ask your daughter-turned-bride if she has any preferences concerning your dress, she'll likely answer in an offhand way, reassuring you that the MOB dress is totally your domain, completely up to you. But within thirty seconds, she may have more to say. The conversation will probably go something like this:

"Mom, now that I think about it, you might want to look for a floor-length dress since the bridesmaids' dresses will be floor length."

"Well," you'll say, hesitating, "I might not be able to wear it again, but I see your point. Okay, I'll shop for floor length."

"And what color are you thinking about?" she'll ask.

That's when you'll chuckle and answer, "What color do you *want* me to think about?" She'll smile and protest a bit and then together you'll discuss some options.

Suddenly the focus has shifted ever so slightly from *it's all about me* to *whatever I want—with the bride's approval*. It is, in fact, her day and her vision. Your all-about-me party didn't last long, but you can live with that. You're a mom. You're used to it. As moms, we set aside many of our own plans and desires every day to do what's best for our kids. And we'll be doing it till the day we die.

But for now it's time to shop—or sew, for any who choose that route. Why not make it fun and start with a squeal—if you've still got one in you at this point! Invite a friend or sister along on this special shopping expedition and make a day of it. Your husband will thank you for not involving him, and after all, it's really for the best. He'd wilt within an hour or two and then tell you that you look good in the next thing you try on.

Your daughters may not even be the best shopping buddies for this particular mission. If they're anything like my girls, they may pooh-pooh the things you like and push for something you're not comfortable wearing. Kristin and Kelli even got silly and shoved a few ridiculous options through the fitting room door, making me try them on and parade around in them while they laughed. Ah, the timeless dynamic of the mother-daughter relationship.

Yes, Mother of the Bride, your best bet for this almost-all-about-you shopping task lies in a friend or a sister. Save your family for the final vote of approval or to help you select a winner when you narrow it down to two or three choices.

But first you've got to find at least one choice—and it probably won't be easy. In fact, expect frustrations. If you're aware of potential roadblocks, you can mentally prepare for them and hopefully diffuse some of the stress that will try to hijack your joy.

I faced a challenge that complicated the whole process. Since I live seventy-five miles from the nearest big-city shopping center, the search for a dress truly became a quest. Having only a few opportunities to find a suitable dress placed an extra measure of stress on this specific wedding-planning chore.

Getting to the dress shops may not be a problem for you, but every mother of the bride has color and style issues to contend with. Not only will you have to search for a dress in a color that blends with the wedding colors, but you'll be looking for a style appropriate for the season and also the type of wedding, whether formal, beach, afternoon, or evening.

Of course, you'll also want a dress that flatters you. Finding one can become nearly impossible when two or three predominant colors or a trendy style seem to rule the current fashion world. While I was on the dress hunt for Kelli's wedding, the ruffle rage met me at every turn. I pressed on, though, until I found something that could stand the test of time—and the permanent record of photo albums.

When you *do* find the color and style you want, MOB, be

prepared for other difficulties—namely the price. If you're like me, you're naturally drawn to the most expensive options out there. Try not to pass out when you check the price tag of the dress that's especially stunning on you. If you must—and I had to as a first-time MOB—continue looking while you keep this beauty in mind. You may eventually return to the more expensive option to be happy with your final selection—as I did—but at least you'll know you didn't make a hasty decision. You'll be able to move forward with excitement instead of guilt.

Another strategy is to purchase an in-the-meantime dress. With distance and lack of shopping opportunities hanging over my head, I didn't want to be caught with my girls' weddings a week away and still no dress. Instead, for each girl's wedding I bought a this-could-work-but-I'm-not-crazy-about-it dress. If I found something I liked better, I returned the runner-up. If you decide to do this, be sure to check the *return by* date. You don't want to pay for a second dress—especially at MOB dress prices.

Once you've found the perfect dress, be prepared for another possible roadblock. They may not have your size. At this point you'll think an evil plot is afoot to drive you the last few feet toward crazy, but if you have time on your side, you might be able to order the right size. Even then a problem could occur. I had to order one of my dresses twice before I got one in good condition. Take my word for it: if your dress arrives with a spot or snag on it, you may need to order a straitjacket next!

After you know your selection is final, be sure to update the mother of the groom. She'll need to know the color and style you chose so she can follow suit and select a dress that will coordinate well with your choice as well as the general colors of the wedding. She will appreciate getting the information, and it could also prevent an unpleasant clash of colors the day of the wedding.

Even after you have your dress in hand, you may be met with another challenge. I had to have both of mine altered before they fit properly. It's a good idea to allow extra time—and money—for this possible scenario. Just take a deep breath and press on through this as well. The frustrations you encounter while finding your dress will be a distant memory on the wedding day.

Once you've achieved success on the MOB dress front—and don't forget the shoes and purse to match—you'll feel reenergized. You might even want to squeal again. I say go for it. Relax and enjoy your beautiful new dress. You deserve it.

Yes, you, Mother of the Bride, are an important part of the wedding. You get to look gorgeous too. Delight in your MOB outfit. Enjoy wearing that knockout dress, that little splurge on you. It's time for you to shine!

A Gem for the Journey

Acknowledge your importance as a mother of the bride and allow yourself to shine.

Treat Yourself

Buy the dress you love. You're the mother of the bride. You deserve to look your best!

Talk It Over

Call the mother of the groom or get together for coffee and fill her in on what style and color of dress you're planning to wear. Offer tips to one another on the best places to find dresses and accessories. You could even discuss how you want to wear your hair and whom you might have style it.

A Bonus Wedding Planning Tip

Take a nice pair of comfy sandals, flip-flops, or slippers with you on the wedding day to wear before the ceremony and as the reception winds down. Have fun color coordinating them with your dress. Also, if your funds are quite limited, upscale resale shops can be the perfect place to find gorgeous MOB dresses at prices you can afford.

Your MOB Musings

Some of my concerns about my appearance on my daughter's big day are:

_____

_____

_____

_____

_____

_____

_____

_____

_____

_____

_____

_____

_____

_____

A Day to Remember: Getting a Sneak Peek

It's no secret. All wedding-planning tasks are not created equal. A few rise above and beyond when figuring in the thrill factor. Shopping for a wedding gown certainly vies for the lead, but bridal portrait day claims a top spot as well. My daughters' bridal portraits were no exception. What I didn't expect, though, were the glitches that added to the adventure—and memory—of it all.

Midway through Kristin's hair appointment on her special day, she and I stole nervous glances at each other. The photographer had reserved an hour time slot at The Tulsa Garden Center for the photo shoot that afternoon, but would we make it on time? The deeper the hairdresser got into Kristin's thick head of hair, the more obvious it became that we faced a race against the clock.

"How much longer do you think it will take?" I asked Kendall, Kristin's stylist at the Ihloff Salon. "We've got to be at the Garden Center by four."

"And I need time to get dressed and have Kelli do my makeup," Kristin added. We didn't want Kelli—sister, maid of honor, and makeup artist for the day—forced into a rush job for this once-in-a-lifetime event.

"I didn't anticipate it taking this long," Kendall said, "but Kristin, your hair is so thick. The layers just seem to multiply." As she lifted another section of hair and secured it with a clip, she said, "I'll do the best I can. I think we can have you there on time."

I had so yearned for everything to go well for this special prewedding experience. Since a ten-hour drive normally separated Kristin and me, so much of our other planning had to be crammed into short, jam-packed visits. Even our wedding planning had to be planned. I longed for this day to be different—to be more relaxed, to be worry-free.

The day started out smoothly enough. We had arranged for Kristin's bridal portrait to be done while she visited first Shawn and then us for spring break. Even so, Kristin, Kelli, and I found ourselves in three different states when portrait day arrived.

We each drove to Tulsa, planning to meet at the florist shop to make final arrangements there. I, however, needed to drop the bridal gown off at my sister's workplace first. No reason to chance having the dress stolen out of my car while we tended to errands. Besides, Carolyn was happy to play Keeper of the Gown. It perked up the stuffy, all-business atmosphere she and the other bank employees usually had to maintain.

After giving Carolyn a peek at the dress and making plans to pick it up later that afternoon, I hurried to the florist shop. I wanted to have ample time to take care of business and then have a leisurely lunch somewhere special with my girls before Kristin's hair appointment. I wanted this to be a day to remember.

Kristin and I arrived at the shop at nearly the same time and jumped out of our cars, grinning from ear to ear. "Can you believe it's bridal portrait day? Can you believe we're about to choose your flowers?" I said as I gave her a hug. She just laughed. The sunshine and blue skies of the beautiful spring day perfectly reflected our spirits.

Once inside, with a multitude of choices before us, I realized this would take longer than we first anticipated. When Kelli came breezing in, she found us elbow deep in catalogues and wedding albums. As the minutes ticked by, I wanted to move ahead with our lunch plans, but we needed to stick to business and finalize the floral arrangements. Kristin would not be in Tulsa again before her wedding weekend.

As we left the shop, the sun was still shining, but our spirits had begun to droop. At least mine had. "Girls, I really wanted to treat you to a special lunch today, but now I'm concerned about the time. I wonder if there's a nice restaurant nearby."

"I think something quick will have to do," Kristin said. "I don't want to be late for my hair appointment."

Thus began the glitches that threatened to put a damper on my day-to-remember dreams. And now, even though we had inhaled a fast-food lunch to make it to the salon on time, we found ourselves racing against the clock again. As Kendall pinned the tiara and veil in place, Kristin suggested another change in plans. "Mom, I think Kelli and I should go on to the Garden Center while you pick up the gown. She can get my makeup done, and then I'll be ready to get dressed as soon as you get there."

"But Carolyn wanted to see you," I said, though I was

thinking of myself as well. I didn't want to miss a minute of the fun, a minute of getting the bride ready. I also had never been to the Garden Center and was worried about finding it by myself on time.

Kristin was right, though. We didn't have a choice. As the girls hurried to Kelli's car, with Kristin sporting her wedding veil and tiara, I looked on from afar. No time to sulk, though. I had a job to do.

Luckily, the bank was only blocks from the salon. After grabbing the dress and making the girls' apologies, I flew to the Garden Center, missing only one turn along the way. With not a minute to spare, I dashed inside—as fast as a mother of the bride *can* dash while carrying a full-length bridal gown—and spotted Kelli standing as lookout and waving me toward the makeshift dressing room.

Like a heroine rushing in to save the day, I swooped through the dressing room door, precious cargo in hand. Kristin, already in her slip, was ready to jump into the gown as soon as I could get it out of the bag. We all moved quickly but with the utmost care in protecting the dress. We wanted it kept perfect for the wedding.

As Kelli and I carried the train of Kristin's gown and trailed her out of the dressing room, the photographer directed us to a room encircled with windows and filled with afternoon sunlight. Kelli and I had played our roles in getting the bride-to-be ready, and now Chris, the photographer, stepped in to play his.

After Chris got Kristin set for the first shot, I finally gave myself permission to take a deep breath and relax. And then there it was. The moment my spirit longed for, my day-to-remember dreams coming true. I got my first real look at my daughter as a bride.

I could say that she was beautiful, but *beautiful* falls short of describing what I saw. My Kristin, my little girl, looked more radiant than anything my eyes had ever beheld. Her eyes danced. Her smile told the story. She was a woman in love and ready to get married. With a breathtaking beauty nothing could have prepared me for, she moved my heart to a new depth of joy. She made it a day to remember.

When I could trust myself to speak, with hushed voice I said to Kelli, "Look at her. She's gorgeous."

"I know," Kelli answered, touched by the scene herself.

"If your dad was here, he'd be bawling," I said. We looked at each other and smiled. "I wish Carolyn was here. She would have loved this."

I certainly loved it. Loved getting a sneak peek of the joy that awaited us on wedding day. God lavished such blessing on me during those precious moments. My heart would surely burst on the big day itself.

The minutes flew by as we followed Chris and Kristin from room to room and eventually outside. Chris even asked me to help with a few shots. I smiled and jumped into action, delighted to play a part in capturing my daughter's beauty as a bride.

After the photo shoot ended, one more change of plans developed. "Kristin, why don't you leave your veil on, and we'll run back to the bank so Carolyn can see you in it."

The girls looked at me like I'd lost my mind, but they soon got caught up in the adventure of it all. Kristin caused quite a stir, walking into the bank in a wedding veil and tiara. A few of the stuffed shirts shot disapproving glances our way, but Carolyn and her female coworkers immediately flocked around us. Ah, the sisterhood of weddings. Certain things are common to all.

And thus ended our bridal portrait day. A day to remember. A day for sneak peeks and savored moments. Moments I'll hold forever as snapshot images in my heart.

Every mother of the bride deserves to have such a day. Yours, MOB, may or may not involve a bridal portrait session. Your day to remember might unfold as your daughter tries on wedding gowns or as she and your husband practice their father-daughter dance. It might even happen after the wedding rehearsal, as she and your future son-in-law walk out of the church hand in hand, enjoying private conversation and filled with the promise of the morrow.

You'll know it when it happens—your day to remember. Let the rest of the world fall away and take it in. Enjoy it to the fullest, Mother of the Bride, and take a few snapshot images of your own.

A Gem for the Journey

When your dreams for a particular event seem to be slipping away, don't despair. An unexpected joy may be waiting in the wings.

Treat Yourself

Pull out your wedding album and slip back in time. Become a bride again for a few minutes.

Talk It Over

Tell the bride-to-be about the moments you most treasure from your wedding-planning days with her and then together offer a prayer of thanks to God for blessing you with such sweet memories.

A Bonus Wedding Planning Tip

Take a clean white sheet for your daughter to stand on as she gets dressed for her bridal portrait. Also carry the bottom portion of the gown as she moves from place to place and gets set for each series of photos.

Your MOB Musings

Some of the moments I most want to remember from our wedding-planning days are:

_____

_____

_____

_____

_____

_____

_____

_____

_____

_____

_____

_____

_____

_____

_____

_____

_____

Shower Her with Fun:
Time for Some Joy

"IT IS A HAPPY TALENT TO KNOW HOW TO PLAY."
—RALPH WALDO EMERSON

If you ever want to speed up time, all you need to do is schedule a wedding. Months will feel like moments, and days will disappear. Before you know it, you'll find yourself only a couple of months away from the big day. When that happens, Mother of the Bride, the word *busy* gets redefined. I hate to say it, but things might even get tense.

As strain mounts, it's the perfect time for you and your daughter to infuse some joy into your lives. Why not let her bridal showers provide that? Kick back, have fun, and enjoy the girly delights that bridal showers offer. And, MOB, do your part to make the festivities as happy and memorable as possible for your baby-girl-turned-bride.

I wish I could tell you that her bridal showers will be completely joyful and stress-free for you, but that wouldn't be quite true. Before we look at the joys, let's consider some challenges you might encounter. Some of the stressors could be social while others may be emotional. A few might even involve more work. The good news? You can handle them all.

The first twinge of stress might hit as you contemplate a shower gift. As much as you hate to admit it, you may feel driven to give a gift as good as the groom's parents give. Instead, use the bridal shower as a prime opportunity to squelch any competitive streaks you may have percolating in your heart (more on that later).

If your gift is modest and you're worried about what people may think, let me put your mind at ease. Everyone, including the bride and groom, understands that you have major expenses right now. You can give a thoughtful gift with a theme, like Christmas items or pretty frames for wedding pictures. Another option might be something the newly married couple can use at the reception, such as elegant toasting flutes or a beautiful cake knife and server set. Just give a gift from the heart—something you choose with care—and the bridal couple will remember it with love.

Another challenge may be the need to help hostess a shower for your daughter. Since both of our girls had lived away from home for a few years before they married, their bridesmaids and close friends were no longer local. In order for them to have showers here at home, I needed to help organize them.

Of course, the last thing a mother of the bride needs is more work, but if you find yourself in a similar situation, do as I did and recruit plenty of help. Ask your best friends, family members, and the bridesmaids who are able to attend to help hostess the event and then divide the tasks among yourselves. However, during the shower, have the other hostesses be in charge of everything so you can fully enjoy your mother of the bride role.

Even though the shower might require some work on your part, enjoy the preparations. Here's *your* chance to choose the colors and a cake. Have fun making the shower an unforgettable memory for your sweet daughter. If possible, plan a surprise element—something that will make the event even more special for her. We asked everyone to bring their favorite recipes to help Kristin and Kelli build their cooking repertoires. Some would call that newlywed gold.

Another challenge that may surface the day of the shower could be a disappointing turnout. Friends or relatives you hoped would attend may not come after all. Since a bridal shower is an opportunity to show love and support to the bride and groom— and their parents as well—it can hurt when friends or family choose not to attend. Even though you know everyone has busy schedules, it still stings when they don't take time to come and celebrate with you and your daughter.

If this happens to you, try not to let disappointment steal the happiness of the day. Instead, celebrate fully with those attending and do your best to make it an unbridled time of joy for your darling girl. And as for those who let you down, take the high road and encourage your daughter to do the same. Forgiveness is always the better way.

In addition to the bridal shower on your side of the family, the groom's family will likely host a shower as well. Either their party or yours may present you with one of your first opportunities to socialize with them. You may even find yourselves in one another's homes for the first time.

As you get to know your daughter's in-laws-to-be, you may struggle with comparing yourselves to them. It happened to me when our daughters got married. Such a reaction is natural when our baby girls join new families. Even though the comparison tendency is to be expected, it's never wise. Be alert to competitive or jealous feelings that pop up, and do your best to quickly reject them. Keep in mind that you'll both bless the couple in your own unique ways.

On the day of the shower, go ahead and toss any insecurities or fears on the back burner and concentrate on making the day relaxed and wonderful for everyone. In fact, take advantage of the opportunity to get to know the groom's family and friends better. After all, they'll be in your daughter's life—and sometimes yours—for the rest of your lives. As mother of the bride, do your best to help members of both families mingle and feel comfortable with one another. As in so many aspects of the wedding preparations and events, your demeanor may set the tone for the entire group.

In spite of whatever challenges you might face on this shower-your-daughter-with-fun day, rest assured that the joys are greater. It's so much fun to watch your daughter and the love of her life begin to accumulate treasures for their first home together. And what a treat to soak up the feminine atmosphere and beauty of a bridal shower. Let it refresh you in the midst of crunch time.

Celebrating with friends and family and building your budding relationship with the in-laws will also refill your joy tank. Plus, a joy all its own comes when dear ones give meaningful gifts to your kids. Both Kristin and Kelli received gorgeous handmade quilts from a longtime family friend, and an elderly neighbor gave them Hummel figurines from her personal collection. Gifts like these become family treasures as soon as they're received. To top it off, giving *your* gift delights your heart as well.

Memorable moments that unfold will provide the icing on

the cake of your bridal shower joys. These might happen during silly shower games or when the groom drops in to say hello and sample a piece of cake. My dad even attended one of Kristin's showers and prompted plenty of smiles when he tried to make off with a waffle maker. When it came time for Kelli's bridal shower, my mom added to the memories by accidentally leaving their gift at home, three hours and a state away.

So, Mother of the Bride, as you shower your daughter with fun, don't be surprised when these special parties bless you as well. Consider it a preview of the joy, fun, and memories awaiting you during the wedding weekend. So go ahead, give it your all. Minimize the stressors and fully experience the joy. Relax and have fun!

A Gem for the Journey

Say no to stress and concentrate instead on having fun and giving joy.

Treat Yourself

Be a girly girl for the shower. Wear something that makes you feel pretty—a dynamite top, a stylish dress, or a cute pair of shoes.

Talk It Over

Brainstorm with the bridesmaids and other hostesses for your daughter's shower to come up with ideas and activities that will make the event especially fun and memorable for your beloved girl.

A Bonus Wedding Planning Tip

Ask everyone at the shower to introduce themselves by telling how long they've known the bride and what role they play in her life. This great icebreaker always leads to smiles.

Your MOB Musings

The joys I'm especially looking forward to during the bridal shower and the stressors that I'm dealing with include:

_____

_____

_____

_____

_____

_____

_____

_____

_____

_____

_____

_____

_____

_____

_____

_____

_____

Coming Down the Homestretch: Make a List and Hang On

"AND LET US RUN WITH PERSEVERANCE THE RACE
MARKED OUT FOR US ..." —HEBREWS 12:1 NIV

Mother of the Bride, remember the months that stretched before you after your daughter and her fiancé set their wedding date? Now the months have dwindled to mere weeks, and you're asking yourself two questions: *How can we possibly get everything done? And where will I get the strength to finish this crazy mother-of-the-bride race?*

You're not alone. Every MOB who helps plan her daughter's wedding asks herself the same questions. After all, the last six to eight weeks before the big day will demand the physical, mental, and emotional fortitude of a marathon runner.

As mother of the bride, you'll have three major jobs to do as you come down the homestretch: 1) Keep everything running smoothly, 2) Troubleshoot, and 3) Keep the bride sane—along with yourself. Almost everything that happens will fall into one of these categories, but not necessarily in this order. Each day will birth its own priority.

How did I keep things running smoothly during my homestretch days? I wrote everything down—everything from guaranteeing the number of guests with the caterer to finding white extension cords to redoing the nail polish on my toes. My to-do list took on a life of its own. As soon as I checked off an item, I'd have to add three more. Even though my list seemed to run *me* at times, I couldn't have managed without it. I lived and breathed by it. It kept me on track and organized. In fact, my list may have been the thing that kept me sane.

Only mother-of-the-bride veterans can fully understand the multitude of tasks that need to be coordinated during those final weeks. Since many weddings also serve as family reunion weekends, the MOB has not only wedding details to manage but arrangements and activities for out-of-town family members as well.

Let's think about wedding plans first. As mother of the bride, you'll likely be the one to confirm final decisions and times with vendors, make payments on schedule, keep track of RSVPs, have the wedding gown steamed, shop for your own attire, and even select photos from more than twenty years of albums for the photo tables and slide show.

You might also be up to your MOB neck in planning reception seating, making some of the décor, providing itineraries or lists for the appropriate people, having the bridal portrait framed, getting the programs printed, and any number of other tasks the bride doesn't have the time or the steady nerves to handle. The list goes on and on.

Since both of our daughters' weddings took place out of state, I also had to pack everything needed. As if that wasn't enough, in the weeks preceding Kelli's wedding, my mother-in-law's serious health crisis heaped hospital and caregiving duties on my shoulders as well. Mother of the Bride, you too may face unique or unexpected challenges during your homestretch. That's when you dig deep for your second wind and press on.

On top of wedding details, arrangements also need to be made for out-of-town family. You may wonder if this will be the straw that breaks the mother of the bride's back, but try not to worry. By this point, you will have become an organizational maven on steroids, and you *will* be able to handle it.

Here's what you can do: If hosting houseguests, plan ahead, cook ahead, and clean ahead. Better yet, bring food in and hire a cleaning service if your budget allows. If hotels are needed, research available options and find the best fit for your family. Then send everyone the accommodations information along with an itinerary of events. It's also helpful to compile a list of possible activities for their free time. Since they've invested time and money to attend the biggest day of your little girl's life, you want everyone to have an enjoyable reunion and mini-vacation.

Never be afraid to ask for help. If you're lucky like me, you'll have an expert organizer in the family who'll be happy to knock out a few lists and send some e-mails. A good mantra for any MOB is, "If someone else can do it, let them." There will be plenty that only you can do.

That brings us to your second homestretch job, MOB—troubleshooting. Problems invariably pop up as you attempt to keep all the cogs of the upcoming extravaganza running smoothly.

A few weeks before Kristin's wedding, we barely survived the wedding-gown-cleaning woes. For Kelli's wedding, printing issues with the invitations and programs plagued us. I nearly turned in my MOB badge over that ordeal. Just when you think things can't get more ridiculous, somehow they do.

To make matters worse, many of the problems won't happen until the last week—or hours—before the wedding. When Kristin tried on her bridal jewelry with her gown just days before the wedding, we discovered her necklace was too long. Even though our local jeweler shortened it for us on short notice, we discovered the day of the wedding that it still hung too low for Kristin's dress. With no time left to fix it, we decided to tape the excess to the back of her neck and hide it under her long hair. Crazy but true.

It's hard to tell what coming-down-the-homestretch crises may come *your* way, MOB, but come they will. We experienced everything from jewelry issues to tent card problems, from wrong tablecloths to a missing silver purse, from not enough yellow M&Ms for one wedding to not enough truffles for the other. Be encouraged, though. We pushed through and resolved each problem—and I gained only a few gray hairs in the process.

Finally, Mother of the Bride, your third major homestretch duty will be keeping the bride sane. All of those last-minute problems can and will drive your darling daughter past her limits unless you're there to absorb the brunt of the stress. In fact, if you're doing a good job in your troubleshooting role, you'll be fulfilling your sanity-saving role as well. Every time you troubleshoot a problem, you'll also be protecting your daughter's peace of mind.

A simple Band-Aid helped me keep Kristin sane when the last-minute crisis with her necklace struck. During those same days, when handwritten names on the tent cards didn't look professional no matter how carefully she wrote, Kristin pressed on like a crazed woman. She didn't know what else to do since time was running out. I finally said, "Kristin, stop. Let's stop and think." I reminded her of our friends whose office supply store offered printing services. "I know it's last minute, but I bet they'll help us." And they did. Once again, I protected the bride's sanity.

In another sanity-saving measure, I tried to provide a calm atmosphere for my girls on their wedding days. I didn't accomplish it perfectly, but I did my best to keep the hours leading up to the wedding as private and relaxed as possible. No need to stress over mingling with extended family or friends before the ceremony. There would be plenty of time for that at the reception.

And, Mother of the Bride, in the midst of taking care of everyone and everything else, try to protect your own sanity too. This can be hard to do when it's sink-or-swim time, but if *you* go down, the ship just might go with you. Living by my MOB to-do list helped keep me sane during my homestretch weeks. That and a lot of prayer. Not only my own prayers, but I asked my sisters and best friends to pray as well. Just days before Kelli's wedding, I e-mailed my friend Teri with this request:

For some reason this morning, I've been feeling anxious and almost panicky—no real reason, things are fairly well under control, but I do still have lots of tasks to do. Maybe it's because I feel such a sense of deadline now. I sure wish everything was done so I could relax the next couple of days, but it looks like I'll be busy until we leave. I'm sure Kelli is feeling the same way. Please pray that we'll feel at ease even in the midst of the last-minute duties. I know once we get there, we'll have great fun meeting up with family and enjoying the weekend. Getting there is the problem!

If getting there feels pretty overwhelming in your homestretch days, MOB, remember that I felt it too. It's only

natural. This is probably the biggest event you've ever planned—
or will plan—in your life.

My advice? Make your list, remember to delegate, and then
hang on. It will be worth it all the day you give the gift of a
wonderful wedding celebration to your precious daughter and
her Prince Charming. For now, run the race with perseverance,
Momma.

A Gem for the Journey

Live by your list and don't be afraid to ask for help.

Treat Yourself

Take a much-needed Sunday afternoon nap and then schedule some fun days for sometime after the wedding.

Talk It Over

Call or e-mail your best friend and unload your feelings freely. If she is a woman of faith, tell her some specific ways she can be praying for you during your homestretch days. Be strengthened by the support she offers.

A Bonus Wedding Planning Tip

If you're using framed photos as décor, plan ahead with your daughter exactly where the photos will be placed so you can carry this out on decorating day without stress. If you're doing a photo table, it's even helpful to practice setting up the photos at home first.

Your MOB Musings

When I'm feeling especially overwhelmed with wedding planning, some things that help me are:

And Then There Were Tears:
Expect a Meltdown

"IF YOU HAVE TEARS, PREPARE TO SHED THEM NOW."
—WILLIAM SHAKESPEARE

Mother of the Bride, your goal is now in sight. The wedding weekend has arrived, and your treasured daughter will soon become a wedded wife—but not before a few more surprises. Be prepared, because one in particular has your name on it. A meltdown is headed your way, and it could happen at any moment.

We've all heard that forewarned is forearmed, but that's not necessarily true where the MOB Meltdown is concerned. To be honest, you probably can't avoid it, but at least I can help prepare you for the puddle of tears that's on your horizon. I can give you the best strategy I know for dealing with the cry fest in your near future. That strategy is simple: *Know that it's coming.*

Most MOB meltdowns get triggered by one of two things—nostalgia or stress overload. And, more specifically, *sleep-*

deprived stress overload. Remember the MOB Brain-Stuck-in-Overdrive malady? It progresses to a whole new level the weekend of the wedding. During the wee hours of the morning on Kristin's wedding day, I finally gave up and got out of bed around 4:30 a.m. to jot down all the last-minute to-dos flying through my mind. Sleep was a lost cause.

However, lost shut-eye and culminating stress didn't tip me over the edge that weekend. Nostalgia did the job instead.

As mentioned in an earlier chapter, I made it all the way to the reception without crying. The day before the wedding, I navigated all our preparations and the rehearsal dinner festivities without any tears. On wedding day, our getting-ready hours also came and went with no meltdown in sight. I even made it through the ceremony and the DVD slide show at the reception without breaking down.

So what prompted my undoing? What turned this outwardly together mother of the bride into an emotion-gripped momma letting her baby go? The father-daughter dance. When Kristin and Don took to the dance floor hand in hand, a lifetime of memories along with the enormity of giving our daughter away swept over me. It wasn't just Kristin and Don out there. It was all three of us. It was a tribute to the life we gave her and the love we shared. It was the last link in the chain of giving her away.

All emotional reserve fell away. Tears poured down my face, and all I could do was sob my apologies to the family members at our table. Yes, the father-daughter dance became my tipping point that weekend—a full-blown MOB Meltdown.

Kelli's wedding weekend dealt me a meltdown of a different sort—the stress-induced variety. Oh, nostalgia had its way with me, too, as Kelli's Uncle Keith performed the ceremony and prayed a heartfelt prayer over his niece and her beloved. What momma wouldn't shed a few tears over that?

No, the real MOB Meltdown happened at the salon just hours before the ceremony. And nostalgia had nothing to do with it. Instead, a rude hair stylist pushed me over the edge.

Since I rarely get more than a simple haircut, I felt a bit apprehensive about getting my hair done. However, I wasn't about to style my own hair for something as important as my daughter's wedding. I swallowed my nerves and went equipped with a good-hair-day photo of myself and instructions to keep my regular style but dress it up with a few extra swirls.

When we arrived, the receptionist introduced Kelli, Kristin, and me to our respective stylists. After seeing my photo and hearing my instructions, my stylist asked, "Do you use product on your hair?"

"Oh, I just use shampoo and curl it with a curling iron. Then I use hair spray."

We chitchatted about various things as she worked. Nothing seemed amiss at first. But as time dragged on, I kept my eyes trained on the mirror in front of me. She curled and styled and curled and styled and reworked the same areas again and again—and it didn't look good. She asked me once more if I used product on my hair, and I answered the same as before, wondering why she would ask again.

Soon Kristin appeared. Her hair was already done. She looked at me with questioning eyes. Mine answered with panic and exasperation. I frantically chewed peppermint gum to settle the upset stomach I'd developed.

Before long, the bride herself joined us with her hair all finished and veil secured. Why was mine taking so long? At this point I said, "I don't like the way it's looking. What do you girls think?"

Kelli braved a response. "The front part doesn't look right," she said, pointing to the problem area. "If that can be fixed, I think it'll be okay."

I asked the stylist to work on that area again and once more gave her instructions on how I wanted my hair to look. "I'll try," she said, "but since you won't let me use product on your hair, I'm having trouble with it."

Kristin and Kelli looked at me with raised eyebrows, clearly wondering how their mother would respond to that remark. With calm but deliberate words, I said, "I never said you *couldn't* use product on my hair. You asked me if I used product, and I told you what I use at home. You never asked, *May I use product on your hair*? Go ahead and use it if you need to."

She huffed and said, "I just wasted all that time then." Shocked by her rude and unprofessional behavior, I reminded her once more of exactly what I'd said. Then we all waited in silence as she went to work again, this time using product.

Luckily, the end result looked good. However, I walked away upset over how the stylist blamed me for the trouble she'd had with my hair. As I paid the bill in the reception area, I thought I should mention her unprofessional behavior. As soon as I broached the topic, weeks of stress along with lack of sleep and the rude treatment of the stylist all combined to bring me to my tipping point. The MOB Meltdown commenced. My voice cracked and the tears started rolling.

The receptionist, surprised and very concerned, darted off to get the manager. My girls stood behind me with jaws dropped, at a loss as to what to do about their got-everything-under-control mother falling apart in a public place.

"Oh my, I'm so sorry," the manager said as she appeared from an adjoining room. "Who was your stylist? What happened?"

With quavering voice, I told my story through tears. "Well, *she* said ... and then *I* said ... and then *she* said ..." Even then, I knew I sounded pitiful. "I'm sorry for crying. It's been a stressful week."

The manager said, "No, I'm sorry this happened. She acted very unprofessionally. We want everyone to have a good experience here. I apologize."

As we walked out, Kristin and Kelli empathized with me, but we all agreed not to talk about it anymore that day. We needed to move forward and fully enjoy the wedding. Still emotional, I did my best to pull myself together. I didn't want to prolong the upset that had already marred the memory of what should have been a happy outing. Thankfully, we went on to have a joyful wedding celebration.

It's hard to tell when *your* tipping point may come, Mother of the Bride, but come it will. Whether nostalgia related or stress induced, the MOB Meltdown *will* pay you a visit during your daughter's wedding weekend. Just remember that it's coming. Don't be shocked by it—and please go easy on yourself when it happens. Every MOB deserves a meltdown or two. After all, we've earned them!

A Gem for the Journey

Tears are cleansing and may be just the release valve you need to help you complete your mother-of-the-bride journey. Let them flow, dry them, and then finish strong.

Treat Yourself

Promise yourself a facial or new makeup item after the wedding. Pamper that tearstained face of yours!

Talk It Over

After your MOB Meltdown is behind you, tell your story to a few friends and/or family members. Enjoy some after-the-fact laughter about it all.

A Bonus Wedding Planning Tip

Two months before the wedding, ask your daughter to find out which bridesmaids want to get their hair done at the same salon the two of you will be using. Check with the mother of the groom and the grandmothers as well. Make those appointments at least six weeks in advance to ensure getting the times and stylists you prefer. If your budget doesn't allow for salon appointments, ask a couple of friends with a flair for styling hair if they'd serve as your stylists for the day. They might even be willing to do a practice session sometime during the weeks before the wedding. See if you can think of a creative yet inexpensive way to thank them.

Your MOB Musings

My MOB meltdown happened when:

_____

_____

_____

_____

_____

_____

_____

_____

_____

_____

_____

_____

_____

_____

_____

_____

_____

_____

Letting It Unfold:
Enjoy the Wedding Weekend

"ON WITH THE DANCE! LET JOY BE UNCONFINED."
—LORD BYRON

After months of planning, shopping, carrying out wedding tasks, and troubleshooting, it's wedding game time. Ready or not, Mother of the Bride, it's time to let it all unfold. Time to enjoy the fruits of your labor and live each second like the once-in-a-lifetime moment it is.

Along with all the traditional moments surrounding a wedding, family reunion moments may be part of the joy as well. Since we don't often see my sister Debbie and her family, all hailing from Arizona and Florida, our daughters' weddings provided the perfect opportunities to gather for a few days of family fun.

Meals together, family catch-up times, amateur photo sessions, and lots of helping hands for wedding prep and post-wedding cleanup definitely create a memorable reunion. A family that pulls off a wedding together can do most anything together!

Not only do families reunite at weddings but so do friends. Since our girls had been out of school for a few years, the gathering of their bridesmaids also served as happy reunions. For Kristin's wedding, only one of her attendants was local. Two traveled from nearby states and two others came from abroad, one from England and one from Ecuador. Kelli's wedding also saw friends reunite. What fun to watch the girls come together to celebrate Kristin's and Kelli's big days with them.

Prewedding events also serve up major helpings of joy and unforgettable moments. Whether the bride and her friends let loose at a bachelorette party or enjoy the feminine touches of a shower or bridesmaids' luncheon, high spirits and happiness reign.

During Kristin's bridesmaids' luncheon, the solution to her wedding-dress dilemma arrived at the restaurant with a flourish. Like the cavalry charging to the rescue, Shawn's mother swept through the restaurant dining room holding aloft the bridal petticoat that would provide the fix to Kristin's suddenly-too-long wedding gown. Score one for the mother of the groom.

The wedding rehearsal also carries an air of jubilant victory. All have survived the preparations to reach this point, and everyone's ready for fun. Jokes and laughter dominate the proceedings while the mother of the bride interjects reminders of everyone's assignments for the next day. Yes, the MOB is still on task.

The rehearsal dinner, though, is a different story. For me, this was where I finally relaxed. At last someone else was in charge. I soaked up every second of it, talking and laughing with family and friends, eating delicious food that I hadn't had to price or select, and catching my desperately needed breath before the next day's events. It was just the refreshment this weary MOB needed. Another home run for the groom's family.

I must be honest, though, and give fair warning. In the midst of all the joy, Mother of the Bride, I'm afraid you'll have to troubleshoot. Not a big surprise, I'm sure, but it's worth mentally preparing for ahead of time. You won't be able to avoid snags to your plans, but you can determine to enjoy the weekend in spite of the glitches. Plan to keep your cool during the challenges, deal with them quickly, then get back to the business of celebrating the happiest weekend of your precious girl's life.

Sometimes challenges occur because of our expectations. For our extended family's first meal together during the days preceding our girls' weddings, I had envisioned how we'd all be seated around a big table, everyone together again, talking and laughing. The restaurants, however, didn't have the same vision. One didn't follow my reservation instructions, and the other simply couldn't accommodate my dream. I discovered the best way to navigate certain challenges is to let go of expectations and go with the flow.

The day before the wedding—decorating day—can deal the mother of the bride one minicrisis after another. My first time around the MOB block, one rental company got our tablecloth order wrong. The next time, the staff at the reception venue wasn't ready for us at the appointed time—and timing is everything on decorating day. For both weddings, we ran into chocolate shortages—the worst kind of crisis. This was when delegating responsibility and relying on help proved to be my salvation as I coordinated multiple time-crunched tasks.

Be encouraged, though, Mother of the Bride. On decorating day, hidden blessings and joys await as well. Seeing everyone work together to create gorgeous settings for both the wedding and the reception warms the MOB heart and also helps keep everyone energized. A few will even go above and beyond. When everyone else deserted me at one point during Kelli's decorating day, my sister Janice and Kelli's soon-to-be mother-in-law, Lisa, hung tight and worked with me until everything was just as I wanted. I'll never forget their stand-by-me faithfulness and help.

Fun memories will also be created on this challenging day. As we decorated for Kristin's wedding, my sister Carolyn gave an off-the-cuff demonstration on how to spot and then eat slightly irregular M&Ms. The video Kelli caught of that moment still makes me laugh. On Kelli's decorating day, an impromptu work crew we dubbed "The Tulle Girls" formed. They couldn't resist striking a leggy pose for a photo. Zany interludes like this get you through the day.

Also unfolding during your daughter's *I do* weekend will be those once-in-a-lifetime moments that melt your heart. Whether it's seeing sweet interactions between the bride and groom, glimpsing loving gestures from others toward the happy couple, special moments you experience with your little girl turned bride, or the hugs both families share immediately following the ceremony, these are the moments your heart captures and replays long after the wedding is over.

I'll never forget helping Kristin with her necklace as she got ready for her groom. Or hearing that Kelli asked for me when a problem arose with bustling her gown. And who could forget the hug Shawn and I shared the first time we saw each other before the ceremony, or the prayer my brother-in-law Keith prayed over Kelli and Jake before he pronounced them husband and wife. And I'll always remember the love Kristin and Shawn showed for Kelli and Jake when they rewrote and performed a song in their honor at the rehearsal dinner and then again—by popular demand—at the reception. These are the moments that make all the months of preparation worth it. Priceless moments. Treasured moments.

And let's not forget the unbridled joy at the reception—the place where the bride finally lets her veil down, the groom loses his jacket, and everyone else celebrates the radiant couple with good food, great company, and scrumptious wedding cake.

Mother of the Bride, so much joy is in store for you during those party hours. Joy you worked tirelessly to help create. Delight in the sheer beauty of it all and feel the soul satisfaction of having made it possible for others to enjoy. Have fun with your family and friends. Make the rounds—play hostess and visit at each table. You and your guests will both be blessed as you welcome everyone and thank them for coming.

Believe it or not, you may not have time to sit and enjoy the food. I didn't. Various duties and visiting with guests distracted me during dinner, but later I was determined to enjoy the cake. I slowed down and savored every bite. And remember, MOBs deserve a piece of both cakes—the wedding cake *and* the groom's cake. Just consider it payment for all your work and consume every crumb in utter abandon. No counting calories on wedding day.

Last but not least, enjoy those classic memorable moments that happen during the reception. Drop any duties and fully focus on every second of the bride and groom's triumphant entry, the storybook DVD slide show, cutting the much-anticipated cake, those emotional first dances, the fun bouquet toss and garter throw, and finally, the happy send-off—the getaway.

While others call out their best wishes, your last exclamation of "Have fun!" will be the brave face you use to cover your mixed emotions as you watch your baby girl ride away into her new life. Sometimes the tug of heartstrings can hurt a little. But thankfully, the deep joy you feel over your daughter's happiness will be greater.

So, Mother of the Bride, when the big weekend finally arrives, fully enjoy all the once-in-a-lifetime moments that await you. Delight in them. Revel in them. Trust that all your plans and work will pay off, and then watch it all unfold. But don't just watch it—live it. Live every second of it. Enjoy!

A Gem for the Journey

Push *pause* when you need to be fully present. Don't let duties rob you of joy in progress.

Treat Yourself

Ask a family member to take photos for you the entire weekend. Live the moments and let someone else capture the memories.

Talk It Over

When the bride and groom return from their honeymoon, get together for some catch-up conversation. Ask them what their most treasured moments are from the wedding weekend and then share yours as well.

A Bonus Wedding Planning Tip

Make a list of photos you want your professional photographer to be sure to take. E-mail it to him or her before the wedding but also bring a copy as a backup on the big day. Don't be caught afterward regretting that certain shots were not captured.

Your MOB Musings

The wedding weekend moments that I will remember forever include:

_____

_____

_____

_____

_____

_____

_____

_____

_____

_____

_____

_____

_____

_____

_____

_____

_____

23

Basking in the Joy: A Mother of the Bride Gives Thanks

"THE LORD HAS DONE GREAT THINGS FOR US, AND WE ARE FILLED WITH JOY." —PSALM 126:3 NIV

The *I dos* have been said, the cake cut, the garter thrown, and the bouquet tossed high. The newlyweds have taken their exit to shouts and waves all around. What's a mother of the bride to do after the last guest leaves and the remnants of the celebration are cleared away? The obvious answer *rest* cries out, but for me something else had to come first. I had to bask in the joy.

Of course, I'd encountered rough spots and challenges along the way, but the joy of the celebrations themselves overshadowed any problem. I couldn't help but relive the details of Kristin's and Kelli's much-anticipated, long-awaited wedding days. After losing sleep for months while planning the particulars, I found myself unable to sleep once more while replaying scene after scene in my mind.

Their special days had turned out just as we'd hoped. The desire of our hearts to give our daughters and their beloveds wonderful wedding celebrations they would remember forever came to pass. God blessed us with dreams come true.

Watching the events come together so beautifully overwhelmed me with joy and gratitude. God answered one prayer after another and granted blessing upon blessing as the wedding weekends unfolded.

Everyone arrived safely, with members of the bridal parties and the family pouring in from all over the United States as well as abroad. Our family stayed healthy and able to fully enjoy the weddings, and Shawn's grandmother even joined us, despite being released from the hospital just hours before his and Kristin's ceremony. We gained access to both reception sites to do all the decorating a day in advance, and to top it off, we experienced sunny weather and hours of memorable family time throughout the respective weekends.

As a mother of the bride, I discovered that a wedding creates the best reunion possible. Our joy doubled when both family and friends came together to celebrate with us. Reunions are usually just for family or just for friends, but a reunion birthed by a wedding is especially sweet because it brings everyone together at one time. What a blessing to introduce members of one group to the other and to watch them join forces to help us carry out our girls' dream weddings.

Seeing family members play special roles in the wedding celebrations thrilled me as well. After witnessing years of normal sisterly clashes, the bond of family love reigned supreme on their wedding days as both Kristin and Kelli served one another as maid or matron of honor.

Not only did Kelli do a superb job as Kristin's makeup artist and manicurist, she also offered a funny and heartwarming toast at the party. Likewise, Kristin helped both Kelli and me in a multitude of ways. She and Shawn also gifted Kelli and Jake with a song—and thus with moments—that will never be forgotten. My heart melted but swelled with pride at the same time as I watched my girls love one another.

Other family members blessed the festivities in meaningful ways as well. My brother-in-law Keith performed both ceremonies, adding a dimension of joy that could never be manufactured by careful planning or finances expended. How many young women get to have a favorite uncle stand before them on their wedding day and lead them in their vows? What sacred moments we witnessed.

The family's personal touch at Kelli's wedding also included her young cousin Gavin serving as ring bearer and her new little sister-in-law Nikki filling the role of flower girl. One was disinterested but willing while the other was to-the-moon-and-back excited. I'll let you guess which was which.

When it was time to party at Kristin's wedding, her fun-loving cousin Aaron acted as emcee for her reception and moved the celebration along like a pro. Yes, having family members involved in key areas of our girls' wedding days made those treasured hours even more memorable.

Other special joys graced our lives as well during those wonderful wedding weekends. We deepened our relationships with our daughters' lovely new in-laws, the beauty of the reception halls amazed us as our plans became reality, the sentimental first dances tugged at our hearts, and we finally got to meet some of Shawn's and Jake's loved ones that we'd only heard about up until that time. The biggest blessing by far, though, of both wedding experiences was seeing our precious daughters joined together forever with the men they love—men who will faithfully love them and always lead their families in honoring God.

The joy of hopes and dreams realized—for the weddings and for my girls—kept my heart soaring long after I slipped back into life as I knew it before becoming a mother of the bride. Day after day, I gave thanks. I marveled at the blessings poured out on us during those incredible days. The wedding weekends undeniably claimed their place among the highlights of my life.

Mother of the Bride, I'm so glad you've taken a peek into my MOB adventures as you experience your own. When *your* wedding weekend is over, I hope you'll take some time like I did to relive your joys, for you too will soon enough slip back into the regular days of ordinary life. For now, though, bask in the joy as long as you can. Now is the time to rejoice.

A Gem for the Journey

Take time to treasure and relive moments from the wedding weekend. Fix them firmly in your heart and mind.

Treat Yourself

In the days to come, enjoy shopping for a special memento—a reminder of your mother of the bride days.

Talk It Over

Spend a few moments thanking God for the many blessings he lavished on you and your loved ones during the wedding weekend. And if you asked friends to pray for you during those days leading up to the big event, be sure to tell them about all the ways God blessed you.

A Bonus Wedding Planning Tip

As you pack wedding supplies away, make a list of the items you have left along with the number of each one. This information will come in handy for your next daughter's wedding or when you want to loan items to a friend.

Your MOB Musings

My heart overflows with thanks for the wedding weekend joys of:

_____

_____

_____

_____

_____

_____

_____

_____

_____

_____

_____

_____

_____

_____

_____

_____

_____

_____

Wedding Vendor Worksheets

The following wedding vendor worksheets will help you and your daughter gain all the necessary information to select the best vendors for her upcoming wedding. You may find answers to some of the questions on the vendors' websites or through other promotional materials, but it's always wise to ask questions directly by calling or meeting with them. Also included are questions to ask the vendors' references.

My publisher has also made the worksheets available as a handy and useable tool at motherofthebridebook.com. You may download the 8 ½ x 11 worksheets for free by entering your e-mail address and password MOB.

Good luck with your plans, Mother of the Bride. I hope the worksheets are a blessing to you!

CEREMONY VENUE WORKSHEET

- What do you charge for a wedding ceremony to be held in your facility?

- What is included in the charge?

- Hours available:

- Chairs/seating:

- Setup/cleanup:

- Sound system – audio and visual:

- Security:

- Hours for decorating, preferably the day before the wedding:

- Other:

- Is payment due in full upon booking? If not, when is the deposit due? Is deposit refundable if we cancel by a certain date?

- When is the balance due?

- How many can comfortably be seated in the facility?

- How many hours prior to the wedding will the heat or air-conditioning be turned on?

- Where do guests park? Is parking free?

- Where are the restrooms the guests may use?

- Are there any items we are not allowed to move? Will you provide a list of all your rules?

- Will a facility employee be on-site to take care of any issues that might develop?

- Will you provide us with references?

- Who will be our contact person? What is his or her phone number and e-mail?

Questions to Ask Ceremony Venue's References

- Did the contact person respond in a timely fashion to your calls and e-mails?

- Was the contact person easy to work with? Did he or she strive to please?

- Did you have any issues with unusual rules?

- Was the venue clean for your event?

- Was the air conditioning/heating system adequate for the venue and functioning properly?

- Were the restrooms in good working order?

- Did the audio/visual equipment work properly?

- Was a venue employee on-site to take care of any issues that might develop?

- Was the facility unlocked and ready at the appointed time?

- Was everything provided/carried out that was agreed upon when payment was made?

- On a scale of 1 to 10, how would you rate this venue and its management?

RECEPTION VENUE WORKSHEET

- What do you charge for the use of your facility? Are there any extra charges?

- What is included in the charge?

- Hours available, including pre-reception deliveries, reception, and cleanup:

- Tables/chairs:

- Setup/cleanup:

- Sound system – audio and visual:

- Dance floor:

- Linens:

- Security:

- Hours for decorating, preferably the day before the wedding:

- Other:

- How much is the deposit? When is it due? Is deposit refundable if we cancel by a certain date?

- When is the balance due?

- How many can comfortably be seated in the reception hall?

- Where do guests park? Is parking free?

- Is there a kitchen available?

- Do you allow alcohol to be served on the premises? Are any special permits required?

- How many hours before the reception will the heat or air conditioning be turned on?

- Where are the restrooms the guests may use?

- Are we free to meet with our caterer on-site at some point before the reception?

- Will a venue employee be on-site to take care of any issues that might develop?

- Will you provide us with references?

- Who will be our contact person? What is his or her phone number and e-mail?

QUESTIONS TO ASK RECEPTION VENUE'S REFERENCES

- Did the contact person respond in a timely fashion to your calls and e-mails?

- Was the contact person easy to work with? Did he or she strive to please?

- Was the venue clean for your event?

- Was the air-conditioning/heating system adequate for the venue and in good working order?

- Did the plumbing work well in the bathrooms and kitchen?

- Did the audiovisual equipment work properly?

- Was a venue employee on-site to take care of any issues that might develop?

- Was setup ready at the appointed time?

- Was everything provided or carried out that was agreed upon when payment was made?

- On a scale of 1 to 10, how would you rate this venue and its management?

PHOTOGRAPHER WORKSHEET

- How would you describe your approach to wedding photography? Do you take formal shots as well as journalistic style photos? Will you take the shots we request?

- How many years of experience do you have? How long have you owned your own business?

- Do you work out of your home or a studio? (Less overhead may mean less expense to you.)

- What is your specialty? (The best wedding photographers specialize in weddings and portraits.)

- How many weddings do you do per year? (Ten to fifteen per year is a good sign.)

- How much do you charge? What packages are available? What is included in each package? (Purchase a package that includes enough photos to tell the story of your wedding day—60–80 shots, including 10–20 enlargements. Also try to get a package with a DVD of all photos included—you buy the rights to all photos.)

- Will you do a custom package for us?

- Will our package price be guaranteed through the date of purchase?

- Is there an extra charge for travel? Any other extra fees?

- Approximately how many photos will you take for the fee charged?

- How much is the deposit? When is the balance due?

- How long do you spend after the ceremony taking pictures before heading to the reception? Will you stay until the going-away photos are shot?

- Do you bring an extra camera in case something goes wrong with the one you're using? Do you have an associate on call if an emergency arises and you can't make it?

- If you have associates, who will take our wedding photos? (Make sure to view the work of the photographer who will be shooting your wedding.)

- How do you print the pictures? Are they archival quality?

- Are your coffee table books printed on sturdy/board-type pages or on paper? May we see an actual album in our package? (Don't sign with a photographer at a bridal show. Ask to meet with him to see more of his work. Visit three to five photographers and look at lots of albums. Look at the details of the photos, especially those taken in low light.)

- Will we be able to view our proofs online or will we receive hard-copy proofs? If hard copy, will they be unmarked? What size? May we purchase them at a discount?

- How soon will the pictures be ready after we place our order?

- Will you provide us with references?

- May we include these items in the contract?

  - Name and phone number of photographer

  - When he will arrive, how long he will stay

  - Minimum number of proofs

  - Exact number of prints and type of album

  - Exact date proofs will be ready and date final album will be delivered

  - Provision in case he gets sick or can't make it

  - Specific dates of deposit and final payment

  - Any additional charges for travel, overtime, costs, other fees

- Question for you, the couple, to ask yourselves: Do we like him or her? (You will be spending lots of time with him—engagement and bridal portrait sessions, the wedding day, contact after the wedding when choosing photos, placing orders, etc.)

Questions to Ask Photographer's References

- Was the photographer on time for appointments and photo shoots?

- Did he respond to phone calls and e-mails in a timely fashion?

- Was he pleasant to work with?

- Were you happy with your photos and photo book? Anything you were unhappy with?

- Did he take the total number of photos advertised in your package? Did he take all the specific shots you asked him to?

- How soon after the wedding did he have the proofs ready to view?

- Did he deliver everything that was agreed upon? Did you get your photos at the agreed-upon time? Did he follow through on verbal statements?

- If you had to do it over again, would you still use him for your wedding?

- On a scale of 1 to 10, how would you rank him?

- Did you know him personally before using him for your wedding?

Caterer Worksheet

- How long have you been in the catering business?

- Are you licensed? Do you have insurance?

- How do you figure your charge? Per person or per item?

- Is it cheaper to order by the item instead of per person?

- What menu items may we choose from?

- Do you specialize in a certain cuisine or menu? Which menu items have proven to be a hit?

- What can you do for $ per person? For $ per person? For $ per person?

- Do you tax only food and beverage and not service?

- Will you match a figure or a menu another caterer has offered?

- Do you provide a written estimate and contract? Will you guarantee price estimates?

- How much is the deposit? When is the balance due?

- May we see actual photos of your work? May we see one of your weddings during setup?

- May we have a taste test of the foods on our menu?

- Where is the food prepared? Do you use any frozen food that you just heat and serve?

- Will wait staff actually dish up servings or just keep food and drink replenished?

- Will servings per guest be limited their first time through the line? Will the food be replenished so guests can have seconds?

- How is the wait staff dressed? How many will there be?

- Is there an extra charge for the wait staff? What is that fee? Any extra charge for cleanup? Do you double charge for labor—fee plus gratuity? May we supply some of our own helpers?

- Do you provide linens and tableware? If so, is that an extra charge?

- When is the menu set in stone? What are your cancellation/ postponement policies?

- Are you familiar with my reception site? Will you be at my event? If not, who is in charge? May I have his or her phone number and e-mail?

- How have you handled receptions where something went wrong?

- Is the wait staff experienced at cutting the cake? Do you charge extra for that? (If so, insist on a low, flat fee, not per guest or per slice.)

- Are we allowed to take the leftovers? Any law preventing it? Will you provide containers?

- Will you get our approval before making any changes or substitutions to the menu?

- Do you receive any commission from services you recommend?

- If you offer cakes, do you make them yourselves or go to an outside baker? Do you charge the customer the same for the cake that you paid for it?

- Do you have an associate on call if an emergency arises and you can't prepare or deliver the food?

Questions to Ask Caterer's References

- How did you know about this caterer?

- Do you know the caterer personally?

- When was the wedding he/she catered for you?

- Did the contact person respond in a timely fashion to your calls and e-mails?

- Did the food taste good? Were hot things hot and cold things cold? Was there always plenty of food and drink available?

- Was the food attractively displayed? Were the serving dishes/utensils in excellent condition? Were the tablecloths, tableware, and napkins nice?

- Were there enough servers? Did they dress and act professionally? Did you see any of the servers eating?

- Was the caterer or food manager there the entire time? If not, who was in charge and did he/she do a good job?

- Was the caterer ready on time? Did she follow your instructions on setup? Did she respond quickly to your requests during the reception? Was she easy to work with overall?

- Did she deliver everything listed in the contract? Did she follow through on verbal statements?

- Did anything go wrong? How did the caterer handle it?

- Did you receive compliments on the reception? What specifically?

- If you had to do it over again, would you still use this caterer?

- If you had to rate this caterer overall from 1 to 10, how would you rate him/her?

Wedding Cake Baker Worksheet

- How long have you been in the wedding cake business?

- How do you figure the cost of the cake?

- Is there a delivery and setup fee? When do you deliver? (Insist on no more than three hours before.)

- Do you charge extra for cake stands, columns, fillings, flowers, etc.? Any other extra charges?

- How much is the deposit? When is the balance due?

- Will you prepare a signed price proposal that details design, flavor of cake and filling, the number it serves, any rentals, delivery and setup fee, deposit info, and delivery date and place?

- Is it cheaper to decorate with flowers? Do you do this or should we ask our florist to do it?

- May we see photos of wedding cakes you've done? (Not just examples from a book.)

- What flavors of cake and filling do you offer?

- May we have a taste test? (The best bakeries will offer these. Don't order without tasting.)

- How far in advance is the cake prepared? (She may have to bake it a few days ahead and freeze it before decorating. Don't go with a baker who freezes cakes for more than a week.)

- How do you make your icing white? (If Crisco is used, the frosting may taste greasy.)

- How do you figure the groom's cake charge? Any additional charge for custom/novelty shape?

- Do you provide boxes or containers for the leftover cake?

- Do you have an associate on call if an emergency arises and you can't bake or deliver the cake?

- Will you provide us with references?

Questions to Ask Wedding Cake Baker's References

- Were you happy with the cake's taste and appearance? Did the baker decorate as directed?

- Did you receive compliments on the cake?

- Was the baker easy to work with?

- Did she return calls and e-mails in a timely fashion?

- Was the cake delivered on time?

- Were the cake stand and any other rentals in excellent condition?

- Did you know her personally before using her for your wedding?

- If you had to do it over again, would you use her to bake your cakes?

- On a scale of 1 to 10, how would you rate this baker?

FLORIST WORKSHEET

- How long have you been in business? Have you done weddings the entire time?

- May we see a price list for wedding flowers?

- Do you have a different price list for regular flowers vs. wedding flowers?

- How much is the deposit? When is the balance due?

- Will you give us a price proposal before the deposit is placed? Do you charge a consult fee for this? (Don't use a florist who charges a consult fee.)

- How many weddings do you normally book for a Saturday during the month of our wedding?

- May we see actual photographs or samples of your work instead of photos in an FTD book?

- Is there a delivery or setup fee?

- Are you familiar with our ceremony and reception sites?

- What time will you arrive at our sites to set up? (Should be no more than two hours prior.)

- Do you stay (or return) to pin the corsages and boutonnieres on the wedding party?

- Do you arrange silk or dried flowers? Are they any cheaper?

- May we view your work during one of your setups before booking you? (Check freshness, beauty, timeliness, etc.)

- What rental items do you have available? What prices do you charge?

- What happens if the flowers we select aren't available on our weekend? Will you tell us the most affordable alternative flowers available and get our okay before preparing them?

- How do you keep the bridal and bridesmaids' bouquets fresh before the ceremony?

- May we preview the flowers the afternoon before the wedding to make sure we like the way you're arranging them?

- Do you have an associate on call if an emergency arises and you can't prepare or deliver the flowers?

- Will you provide us with references?

Questions to Ask Florist's References

- Were you happy with the flowers? Were they fresh and blooming nicely?

- Did the florist prepare the flowers as directed?

- Was he or she easy to work with?

- Did he return calls and e-mails in a timely fashion?

- Did you receive compliments on the flowers?

- Were the flowers delivered at the agreed-upon time?

- Did he deliver everything listed in the contract? Did he follow through on verbal statements?

- Were any extra charges tacked on?

- Were all rental items he provided in excellent condition?

- If changes or substitutions had to be made, did he contact you ahead of time?

- Did you know him personally before using him for your wedding?

- If you had to do it over again, would you use him as your florist?

- On a scale of 1 to 10, how would you rate this florist?

Videographer Worksheet

- How long have you worked as a videographer for weddings?

- How much do you charge to video the wedding and the reception?

- What kind of video camera do you use?

- How many DVDs are included for your fee? How much do you charge for extra DVDs?

- How much is the deposit? When is the balance due?

- Will you provide a contract with all the agreed-upon details listed?

- How many cameras do you use to shoot the wedding?

- Will you and your associates position yourselves well off to the side and at the back during the ceremony? How early will you arrive to set up?

- May we see DVDs of other weddings and receptions you have done? If you have associates, may we see examples from those who will be shooting our wedding? May we have their contact information?

- May we see samples or photos of some of the cases you've done for the DVDs?

- Do you customize the appearance of the discs themselves?

- Will you stay to video all parts of the reception, including the getaway? May we give you a list of the things we want included?

- Will you get footage of our guests and have questions prepared to ask them on camera—favorite stories about the bride and groom, advice, etc.?

- How soon will our video be ready after the wedding?

- Do you have an associate on call if an emergency arises and you can't video our wedding?

- Will you provide us with references?

Questions to Ask Videographer's References

- Were you happy with your video? Were the picture and sound good quality?

- Did the videographer shoot all of the aspects of the wedding and reception that you asked him to?

- Was he easy to work with?

- Did he return calls and e-mails in a timely fashion?

- Did he arrive early enough to set up before the seating of guests started?

- Did he deliver on everything listed in the contract? Did he follow through on verbal statements?

- Did you know him personally before using him for your wedding?

- If you had to do it over again, would you use him as your videographer?

- On a scale of 1 to 10, how would you rate this videographer?

DJ or Live Entertainment Worksheet

- How long have you worked as a DJ (or provided live music) for weddings?

- How much do you charge to DJ (or provide live music) and act as emcee for the reception?

- How much is the deposit? When is the balance due?

- Will you provide a contract with all the agreed-upon details listed?

- Do you provide a playlist so we can select specific songs and/or the type of music we want?

- What kind of equipment do you use?

- Do you practice reading the names of the wedding party? May we call you the week of the wedding to go over the names together so mispronunciations won't occur?

- Will you follow our plan for music and announcements throughout the reception?

- Do you have an associate on call if an emergency arises and you can't make it to our wedding?

- Will you provide us with references?

Questions to Ask DJ's or Live Entertainment's References

- Were you happy with the DJ's (or live entertainment's) performance?

- Did the DJ follow your instructions for music and announcing?

- Was the music too loud or not loud enough? Was the sound quality good?

- Did he do a good job announcing? Was the sound quality of the microphone good?

- Was he easy to work with?

- Did he return calls and e-mails in a timely fashion?

- Did he arrive early enough to set up before the guests arrived?

- Did he deliver on everything listed in the contract? Did he follow through on verbal statements?

- Did you know him personally before using him for your wedding?

- If you had to do it over again, would you use him as your DJ?

- On a scale of 1 to 10, how would you rate this DJ/live entertainment?

Wedding Planner Worksheet

- How long have you been a wedding planner?

- How many weddings have you planned per year for the past three years?

- Do you book more than one wedding for the same weekend?

- What do you charge?

- Would you detail all of your services that are included in your fee?

- Will you provide a contract with all the agreed-upon details listed?

- What deposit is required to secure your services? When is the balance due?

- Will there be any extra charges that are not included in your fee?

- Will you match a competitor's fee?

- May we see photos of some of the weddings you've planned?

- Are you familiar with our ceremony and reception sites?

- Will you get our approval before booking a vendor or spending money for our wedding?

- How often do you stay in touch with your clients?

- How have you handled weddings where something went wrong?

- Do you have an associate on call if an emergency arises and you can't make it to our wedding?

- Will you provide us with references?

Questions to Ask Wedding Planner's References

- Were you happy with how the wedding planner handled everything?

- Did she follow your instructions?

- Was she easy to work with?

- Did she return calls and e-mails in a timely fashion?

- How often did she stay in touch with you and update you?

- Did you receive compliments on the wedding?

- Did she deliver everything listed in the contract? Did she follow through on verbal statements?

- Were any extra charges tacked on?

- Did she get your approval before securing vendors, making decisions, or changing plans?

- Did anything go wrong at your wedding? How did she handle it?

- Were you unhappy with any aspect of her service?

- Did you know her personally before using her for your wedding?

- If you had to do it over again, would you use her as your wedding planner?

- On a scale of 1 to 10, how would you rate this wedding planner?

ABOUT THE AUTHOR

Cheryl Barker is a veteran mother of the bride and freelance writer. She's written for magazines, compilation books, and other publications as well as for Blue Mountain Arts greeting cards, gift books, and calendars. Her heart's desire is to refresh spirits and nourish souls. She and her husband live in Kansas and delight in spending time with their two grown daughters, sons-in-law, and their precious grandchildren. Cheryl loves to take photos, enjoy friends, and indulge in daily doses of chocolate.

motherofthebridebook.com

cherylbarker.net